COLLEGE OF ALAMEDA LIBRARY

WI

D0462811

GV
854.9
C7
T64

Tokle, Art
    The complete guide to
cross-country skiing and
touring

DATE DUE

FEB 06 '74			
DEC 11 '7?			
NOV 12 '7?			
DEC 12 '7?			
JAN 24 '7?			
OCT 10 '8?			
DEC 5 '8?			
OCT 19 '88			

WITHDRAWN

The
Complete Guide
to Cross-Country
Skiing and Touring

The Complete Guide to Cross-Country Skiing and Touring

ART TOKLE AND MARTIN LURAY

Holt, Rinehart and Winston
New York Chicago San Francisco

Copyright © 1973 by Art Tokle and Martin Luray

All rights reserved, including the right to reproduce this book or portions thereof in any form.

Published simultaneously in Canada by Holt, Rinehart and Winston of Canada, Limited.

ISBN: 0-03-001056-X

Library of Congress Catalog Card Number: 72-78119

First Edition

Designer: Margaret Dodd

Printed in the United States of America

For the young people:
Art, Jr., Vivian, Jennifer, and Jonathan
and for their mothers
who provided the encouragement
that made this book possible.

Contents

Acknowledgments

We wish to express our thanks to the following persons who have been extremely helpful in the preparation of this book:

Jakob Vaage, Historian of the Holmenkollen Ski Museum, Oslo, for the pictures used in the first chapter.

Joe Pete Wilson, Per Soerlie, and Johannes von Trapp for the use of the facilities of the Cross-Country Center, Trapp Family Lodge, Stowe, Vt.

Sverre Aamodt, Director of the Sugarbush Inn Cross-Country Center, Waitsfield, Vt., for cooperation in photographing the touring pictures seen in Chapter 6, plus other instructional photos used elsewhere in the book, and to *True* magazine for the use of those photos.

Jim Balfanz, U.S. Nordic Director for his comments and photos of members of the U.S. Olympic Cross-Country Team in action.

Gentlemen's Quarterly for permission to excerpt some material originally written for that publication.

All photos, except where indicated, are by Martin Luray.

Introduction

CROSS-COUNTRY SKIING:
THE BENEFITS OF SILENCE

It is one of those rare days that you hope for in the mountains but hardly ever see. For half a week it has been snowing in the vicinity of Vermont's Mt. Mansfield, and we have been skiing on the flanks of the high peak—most of the time searching out trails protected from the wind and the maelstrom of flying snow.

We have had the usual problems with fogged goggles and falls in the deep stuff and chattering of the ice underneath where the new snow has been scraped away. Bundled in our warm-up pants and parkas and woolen Moriarity hats, we haven't considered it totally unpleasant. By some weird kind of logic peculiar to the Eastern skier, we have been so conditioned that we returned each day to our lodge cold, bruised, and hurting, but still with a dim feeling that we really have been extending ourselves and having fun.

But today is another kind of day. The new snow on the mountain has become puff powder, snow so fine and dry that it dissipates like smoke when you ski through it. The weather is suddenly clear: sunny, bright, but with the bite that denotes temperatures in the pre-teens. I envision the rush down in fresh snow—the exhilarating feeling of speed under control, swooping turns, riding bumps—the whole joyful experience that downhill skiing can be.

I am not, however, on Mt. Mansfield but, regretfully, several miles away standing on a pair of narrow, wooden cross-country skis in the middle of a snow-covered pasture. Everything wobbles: my skis, my low-cut boots. The familiar feeling of control caused by boot fixed to ski is gone. On the other hand, there is an unaccustomed feeling of lightness; the weight my legs have been used to carrying is no longer there, and I shuffle around, tentatively, but rather angrily, knowing that I am missing probably one of the finer skiing days of the season. Still, I have been asked to do a story on cross-country skiing and I am duty-bound to go through with it.

Then Per comes shuffling by, gracefully bounding and sliding, poles flicking, body in fluid motion with a style that I can't help but admire. Within 15 minutes I have begun compensating for the difference between my downhill skis and the new cross-country skis and am absorbing the technique, if not the finished form, of the jogging strides of the touring skier. Then we move off to a trail that takes us out of the pasture and into a pine forest. All is silent except for the huffing of our breath.

Following Per, I find that I'm grooving into the whole thing —the kick–glide–kick–glide rhythm, the feeling of solitude as we pass between the snow-laden conifers. After a mile or so, I begin to understand something about the appeal of cross-country touring. As an alpine skier involved in countering nature's ploys, I have been too busy solving the problems of speed and technique and terrain without taking much enjoyment from the natural world around me. In cross-country, the view narrows down to something more finite: an extreme close-up of what the downhill skier always sees from afar. This becomes especially evident when we stop for a moment to examine some animal tracks. A gray fox has crossed the trail, leaving a single straight line of indentations on the slightly packed surface, then deeper imprints as he plunged into the snow under the firs. Being close to wildlife is one of the small rewards of cross-country skiing—easily as important, I decide, as the constant challenge of danger.

Several hours later, there are other rewards—a mug of hot coffee laced with something alcoholic, a feeling of complete physical warmth, and comfortable tiredness, but not exhaustion. I have put all of my body to use, but I'm not strung out with the tension that comes with downhill skiing. I've been captured by nature for a few hours. Tomorrow I will want to go out again, for a longer run, perhaps making my own tracks. In short, I've been hooked.

This account of my first experience with cross-country skiing several seasons ago was written for *Gentlemen's Quarterly*. I have, since then, found that my experience is not unique. It is typical of what's been happening throughout the United States. Alpine skiers, significantly disturbed by high costs and overcrowding of the slopes, have added another dimension to their sport. Strangely, as you will discover in this book, it has always been with us (what did skiers do before uphill lifts existed?), but the revival of cross-country skiing seems to be another sign of the times, along with the renewed discovery that there is a natural world around us that ought to be preserved.

Cross-country skiers, whether novices or experienced downhillers, are summertime hikers and backpackers. They cherish silence and what Justice William O. Douglas calls "the therapeutic effect of wilderness." They find it hard to understand those, like snowmobilers, who bring their noise with them. No gray fox tracks for the snowmobiler; his treads have crushed them into the snow. He sees naught; silence is his enemy.

This is not to say that I have abandoned alpine skiing. The mountains, too, are therapeutic, and every skier, like the surfer searching for the perfect wave, yearns for that perfect day when the elements are with him, when the elusive combination of sun and light, new snow over a deep, packed powder base exist. Suddenly, at speed, he is able to do everything right on a run that he hopes will never end. I have had a few of those special days and the search continues.

But cross-country skiing means that those perfect days can come even closer together and not necessarily in the Alps or the Rockies, but in the neighboring woods. And this is what this book is all about—to encourage the reader to take part in the sport through its very simplicity. We have eliminated all the nonessentials, in equipment, in technique, and in that old bugaboo, waxing. Credit Art Tokle for this. He comes from Norway, where children literally learn to ski and walk at the same time. He has been a national jumping champion and Olympic jumper and an exceedingly fine alpine skier. Cross-country skiing, however, is his favorite form of relaxation, as anyone who has seen him swing through the forest near his home at Lake Telemark, New Jersey, will testify. Art believes that cross-country skiing is so simple that any reasonably well-coordinated person of any age can learn it in a few hours. After that, it's all joy—a thing between you and your skis and the winter world outside your door.

Summit, N.J.   M.L.
May 1972

The
Complete Guide
to Cross-Country
Skiing and Touring

1 Nordic Skiing

THE NOT-SO-MYSTERIOUS MYSTIQUE

Throughout this book, the terms "Nordic" and "cross-country" skiing and touring are used interchangeably. And well they should, because the modern tourer with his narrow, light skis flicking with a steady pace across the snow-covered terrain is engaging in what may be the oldest form of transportation known to man.

The Nordic peoples, whose Vikings began conquering the sea about A.D. 700, apparently had found a way of conquering their own wild wintry land about 3000 years earlier (Figs. 1 and 2). Remains of primitive skis found above Sweden's Arctic Circle have been carbon-dated to 2000 B.C.

Figure 1. Prehistoric cave drawing found above Arctic Circle indicates ancient inhabitants of Scandinavia may have used skis made of long bones of animals for transportation.

The form of skiing, therefore, in which one travels from point to point over relatively level terrain is named "Nordic" to denote its Scandinavian origins. Alpine skiing, which the Scandinavians call "slalom," is of much more recent vintage. In fact, it is a natural descendant of the Nordic variety; the fork in the family tree occurred in the late nineteenth century, when methods of holding the boot heel to the ski were discovered so that more control could be achieved for handling mountainous slopes in Norway, Switzerland, and central Europe. Ski-jumping, of Scandinavian origin, is also a Nordic winter sport, but it won't concern us in this book.

So, in taking up cross-country, you are reverting to a time when skis were used both as a means of getting about and for sport. Even as late as the twenties and thirties in the Alps and in the United States, one climbed in order to ski down. Venturing into winter made the skier a participant in,

2

Figure 2. According to Norse legend, Ull, son of Odin, traveled about on skis.

if not a celebrant of, the natural world, as Ernest Hemingway observed about skiing in Austria: "I remember the smell
of the pines and the sleeping on the mattresses of beech
leaves in the woodcutters' huts and the skiing through the
forest following the tracks of hares and of foxes. . . . Above
the tree line, I remember following the track of a fox until
I came in sight of him and watching him stand with his right
forefoot raised and then go carefully to stop and then
pounce, and the whiteness and the clutter of a ptarmigan
bursting out of the snow and flying away and over the
ridge."*

Lifts put an end to this. First rope tows, then T-bars,
Pomas, single and double chairs, gondolas, trams laced the
mountains. Suddenly, one had to pay for what he enjoyed
for free before; in the frenzied rush toward the "total resort,"
sight seems to have been lost of the original justification for
skiing as a sport—to strip the urban veneer off for one day
or several and place oneself in conflict with nature. To have
this occur in alpine skiing is rare nowadays, as anyone who
has turned up at certain Eastern resorts during Washington's
Birthday weekend can testify. Add to this the fact that
skiing, which used to be known as "a rich man's sport,"
seems to be rapidly returning to that category, with costs
few families can really afford, and one can understand the
appeal of cross-country. Finally, it seems, the rebellion
against the herd that is taking shape in so many other aspects
of American life is having its effect on winter sports too. Aiding this escape from the mass is the surging interest in ecology.
Cross-country skis are the natural way to view the outdoor
world that one has hiked and backpacked during the summertime.

* "There Is Never Any End to Paris," *A Moveable Feast,* by Ernest
Hemingway, Charles Scribner's Sons, New York, 1964.

If downhill skiers are heading the cross-country trend, beginners are not far behind them, because, for the novice, touring, as opposed to downhill, is relatively simple to learn; the accomplishments possible in the sport take days, not years. The initial taste of skiing is not fraught with fear or tension, since there is little likelihood of accident—yet the joys of being outdoors in winter are retained.

Cross-country skiing does *not* depend upon a number of things. It does not depend upon:

1. A great deal of coordination. If you can walk, you can ski tour.
2. Groomed slopes. Making your own tracks is one of cross-country's great pleasures.
3. Traveling 6 hours on icy highways in order to ski. Golf courses, local woods, parks, country reservations are the haunts of the cross-country skier.
4. Three inches of packed powder over a 50-inch base. If there's 6 inches of fairly good snow—enough to cover what's underneath—you can ski on it. It may be "frozen granular" at your favorite resort because 3000 skiers have wiped off the top surface. But where you'll be skiing, the snow will be untouched and "excellent."
5. Whether the lifts are running in the teeth of a howling wind. What may appear to be a Force 9 gale on the mountain is probably a gentle breeze among the trees below. Which is where you'll be with your cross-country skis.
6. Financing the equipment through your nearest loan association. You can put together a decent cross-country outfit for $60–$80, and we mean everything.
7. Fingers of iron to zip those stretch pants tight. In cross-country, the looser the better. Knickers, knee socks, light anoraks are *de rigeur* if you're *de rigeur*

minded. But literally anything goes, especially if it's dark blue. Lavender hasn't touched cross-country types yet, and probably never will.

It's easy to understand why cross-country appeals to women. What wife and mother doesn't crave the need for silence—to get away by herself for a few hours without being pressed by family demands and sibling quarrels? As opposed to the alpine version of the sport, this is altogether possible in cross-country, with the added plus of no fear of injury. Which explains why women flock to the cross-country centers at major ski resorts—especially on those days when conditions on the mountain tempt only the hardy. For those who prefer togetherness, touring also is very much a family sport. But there is something about the trail that tends to turn off argument. In the silence of the forest, squabbling sounds very loud indeed.

THE SCANDINAVIAN EXPERIENCE

The Scandinavians invented cross-country skiing, and we are indebted to them not only for its ancestry, but for the development of the equipment we use, touring technique, and even for the relatively recent art of waxing.

Skiing in the Scandinavian countries, especially Norway and Sweden, is simply an extension of the way people live. It was always thus, way back to the remote past of the two countries. For all of their small size, both were, and still are, thinly populated. Communication between remote farms and villages during the heavy snows of winter was possible only on skis. Even Norwegian soldiers of the Middle Ages patrolled the countryside on skis. Legends tell of the king's own crack guard, the *Birkebeiners,* transporting the two-year-old heir to the throne out of danger from enemies of the Crown by skiing him to safety hidden behind the shield of one of the soldiers (Fig. 3). Although a fanciful painting of this historic A.D. 1206 event exists, no one really knows how far the soldiers, in their birchbark puttees (hence birch legs, or *Birkebeiners*), traveled on skis. However, an annual race, the *Birkebeiner Lopet,* which commemorates the episode, covers some 40 miles.

The Swedes, not to be outdone, have their own annual commemorative affair, the *Vasaloppet,* probably the most excruciating ski race known to man. It's based on another legend—that of Gustav Vasa, who in 1521 tried to get farmers of the province of Dalarna to revolt against Danish invaders and was snubbed for his pains. Furious at the un-

Figure 3. Fierce *Birkebeiners,* Norwegian soldiers of the Middle Ages, used skis to rescue two-year-old Prince Haakon, heir to the Norwegian throne. Even in A.D. 1206, skiers had their own preferred models. Note differences between skis of the two soldiers.

patriotic Dalarnans, he fled from the town of Mora on skis in an effort to reach the Norwegian frontier. Although modern historians cast doubt on Vasa's skiing prowess, legend has it that he reached Sälen, some 53 miles away, to find a delegation from Mora waiting to plead that he return with them to fight the Danes. Vasa then skied back to lead the successful rebellion that resulted in his becoming King Gustav I. Legend or not, in 1922, the first commemorative Vasaloppet was run from Sälen to Mora with 119 entries, mostly locals. In 1970, the field had grown to a record high of 9000; in 1972, 8000 entered from 16 countries, including a party of 100 Italians. Olympic racers usually lead the pack. In 1972, Swedish Olympian Lars-Arne Bolling won the race in slightly more than 5½ hours, which is considered slow for the 53 miles. The last finisher of the 7200 who finally crossed the line did it in 13 hours, his feet bloodied but his head unbowed.

Long-distance running is a Scandinavian specialty and has very little relationship, other than a family one, to the kind of skiing the recreational tourer usually does. But it is interesting to take note of some of the other accomplishments made by men on skis.

There was, for instance, John (Snowshoe) Thompson, who for 20 years carried the mail on skis across the High Sierras from California to Nevada. Born Jon Torsteinson Rue in Telemark, Norway, in 1829, he emigrated to the United States with his family as a child and moved from Wisconsin to California in 1851, changing his name somewhere along the way. In 1855, after unsuccessfully trying gold mining and raising milk cows, he answered an ad in a Sacramento newspaper calling for someone to carry the U.S. mail over the Sierras to mining camps in Nevada. What possessed him to take the job, no one knows, but for 20 winters this tough Norwegian toted from 60 to 90 pounds of mail from Placerville, California, to Carson City, Nevada, through untracked mountain wilderness on heavy, long skis that he had fashioned himself. The trip today can be made in a matter of hours by car. Thompson usually took 3 full days to do it, subsisting only on beef jerky and biscuits. He slept on the trail at night, holing up during blizzards in a small cave at a halfway point. For 2 decades Snowshoe Thompson was the only wintertime link between California and the Nevada camps, yet, ironically, he was never paid for his services, even though he was backed by California officials in a claim to Washington for $6000 to pay for his hazardous treks. In his 20 years of carrying the mail, it is said he never missed a trip through illness, although he died finally of pneumonia at the age of 49. Atop his grave in Genoa, Nevada, is a pair of skis carved in stone. Thompson has not been forgotten in his native Norway, either; a monument to

Figure 4. Fridjof Nansen traverses Greenland.

9

him stands in the small community of Austbygd in Tinn Parish, Telemark.

Thompson was tough, but even tougher was another Norwegian, Fridjof Nansen, the polar explorer and humanitarian (Fig. 4). In 1888, he and his party crossed Greenland from east to west, covering some 700 miles on skis. In later years, Nansen accomplished other feats in Arctic exploration and was awarded the Nobel Prize for aiding the cause of peace, but his record for cross-country skiing still stands.

CROSS-COUNTRY AS A SPORT: AGAIN THE SCANDINAVIANS

In the early days, skis were purely functional—tools to be used to move people over winter snows that could be crossed in no other way. Rather than isolate themselves during the darkest, coldest time of the year, the Scandinavians had found a way of communicating and staying in social contact with one another. It wasn't until the middle of the nineteenth century that skis were used recreationally; the first cross-country race on skis apparently was held in northern Norway in 1843. The Holmenkollen jumping and cross-country events, on the outskirts of Oslo, are annual affairs now, probably the biggest winter happenings in Norway, with national television and the royal family in attendance. But they are of relatively recent vintage; the first tournament was held in 1892. Waxing was unheard of, and a newspaper of that date reported: "All of the new snow and the sunshine spoiled the day for most of the competitors. As much as six inches of snow was retained on the skis so that some of the competitors appeared to be walking on snowshoes."

These first turn-of-the-century races helped develop cross-country as a sport (Fig. 5). Spectators tired of standing around waiting for the competitors to finish runs that took as many as four hours. So they themselves obtained skis and moved to various vantage points along the track—a custom that is not unfamiliar to us today. Another account of an early Holmenkollen tournament notes that "35,000 pairs of skis are in use in Norway." In advance of that race, one shop in the Norwegian capital had sold out its stock of 500 pairs of skis.

Today, for the true Nordic skier, Scandinavia, especially Norway, is still Mecca. The country is laced with networks of trails that are marked and maintained throughout the winter, encircling not only ski stations and mountain resorts, but the capital as well. It is not unusual to see streams of Oslo office workers, on a dark winter evening, heading for the tram cars that ascend the Holmenkollen, where trails are

Figure 5. Norwegian family on a Sunday outing, about the turn of the century (*Norsk Folkemuseum*).

11

lit for night cross-country running. In the environs of Oslo is the *Nordmarka*—some 1500 miles of marked tracks that plunge deep into the countryside surrounding the capital.

In the mountains and the forests of the country, touring huts dot the landscape. One has a choice of circuits around alpine resorts such as Geilo and Voss as well as remote hotels in the hinterlands that cater only to cross-country tourists. The Scandinavian tourer supplies himself with remarkably well-annotated maps that help him navigate in the snowy wilderness just as National Ocean Survey charts aid the cruising sailor.

The Scandinavian experience had an effect on cross-country skiing in the United States for a long time. But it was imperceptible. While Norwegian immigrants in the Midwest and miners in the Sierras are known to have first used skis for fun before the Civil War, the sport really didn't get started here until 1924, when the first cross-country championships were held in Brattleboro, Vermont. The state is still one of the centers of cross-country activities; Brattleboro's famed Washington's Birthday version of the Vasaloppet, which began in 1963, is an annual affair. Park races and night tournaments, once unheard of, are held frequently in many snowbelt towns.

With the new and sudden spurt of interest in this gentlest of sports, cross-country centers have sprung up in every snowbelt state. There are many miles of maintained trails in the vicinity of most ski communities in Vermont, New Hampshire, and Maine, and acknowledged centers in New York, New Jersey, Pennsylvania, Connecticut, and Massachusetts. The West has them too, in Colorado's Aspen, Steamboat Springs, Vail, Crested Butte, and others, as well as in the Northwest: California's Sierras, Wyoming's Jack-

Figure 6. Everyone skis, including baby, on this trail near Stowe, Vt.

Figure 7. Togetherness on the trail. Cross-country sets no age limits.

son, and Idaho's Sun Valley. So does the Midwest, where cross-country was an early arrival (Fig. 6).

The cross-country centers have the advantage of marked, compacted trails, instruction, rental services, and waxing guidance, and are just the thing for those who want to try out the sport without making a commitment in equipment and clothing. After that, if you live in an area that enjoys the snows of winter, your own home becomes a cross-country center (Fig. 7).

RACING: THE NONRACER AS RACER

Cross-country racing is a specialized version of the sport, but it is more closely allied to the recreational form than downhill racing is to alpine skiing. The mark of a top cross-country racer is enormous stamina—the ability to go any distance from 10 to 50 kilometers at a pace that would destroy the average person. The technique that the cross-country racer uses is, however, closely related to the good touring skier's technique, with one exception—the racer has refined it to the extent of knowing how to handle uphill terrain at speed, how to "rest" on downhill portions, and how to change-up so as to keep from tiring too quickly on level portions. The racer's "kick," as opposed to that of the recreational tourer, provides him with an immense amount of drive—again a refinement of basic touring technique.

The same is not true in alpine racing, where the downhill racer moves at speeds far in excess of anything that the recreational skier can handle safely. Technique is tuned to minute refinements of edge change, body position, weighting–unweighting, and the use of poles and a myriad number of small things that can make the difference of hundredths of a second between winning and being an also-ran.

On the other hand, almost anyone in good physical condition who is willing to run enough cross-country to build some stamina can enter some form of cross-country racing, even if it is only point-to-point touring against a clock. What makes it fun for the adult is that there is no danger involved. Endurance and the smoothing out of technique come with practice and time. For instance, on those days when a lengthy tour is not possible, many cross-country skiers will ski a local course they have laid out with the object of beating their own time. Such a typical circuit should be divided in thirds—one-third gradual uphill, one-third level, and one-third downhill to help sharpen one's ability.

It is not the purpose of this book to deal deeply with cross-country racing other than to illustrate some advanced techniques that racers use that can be utilized by the cross-

15

country tourer to his advantage. It has become evident, however, that the rebirth of cross-country skiing as a recreational activity is leading to new interest in competition among young people. There are a number of junior programs available in the snowbelt states for children 12 years old and up. Until that age is reached, coaching is not as important as interest and having fun. After that, enrollment in a junior program guarantees guidance and a great deal of interclub racing; there are junior races almost every weekend in many areas throughout the country.

Cross-country touring and racing, incidentally, is the ideal secondary school sport. It is not expensive; equipment may be obtained at reasonable cost for the youngsters. It is less injury-ridden than the team sports (the closest parallels are swimming and track) and does not need a great deal of adult supervision. Enjoyment comes not only in the touring and racing, but in the laying out and marking of trails. Cross-country gives an added impetus to the youthful interest in ecology; trails are laid out in the fall and swept free of debris and underbrush. In the winter, when snow is on the ground, the youngsters are not only physically active in an outdoor, rather than indoor, environment, but have the rare treat of viewing another side of the natural world around them firsthand. For children, a touring trip should not be an attempt to get from one point to another in a hurry, but should provide time for discovery. Racing, of course, is another thing, but still, members of the team should be involved in course preparation. They then will have a feeling of total participation.

2 Equipment

LIGHT, LIGHTER, LIGHTEST

When it comes to cross-country equipment, the adage about "form following function" has never been more true. Some basic concepts dictate construction, and the same concepts should rule your choice. Lightness, simplicity, economy, and comfort are the hallmarks of cross-country equipment and clothing; this should overrule every other newly introduced consideration. As an example, there are on the market cross-country skis built of fiberglass and others made of metal that are every bit as expensive as alpine skis. Because economy is one of our guidelines for the selection of equipment (and indeed, what makes cross-country so attractive), there is no reason why the person starting out in the sport should have to dig so deep when the traditional lightweight wood skis are available at about one-fourth the price.

In Nordic skiing, the heel must lift freely to attain the proper on-the-level gliding motion that moves you along the track. For this reason, boots are flexible—either low-cut for racing or higher for general touring. Bindings, too, are simple: modern versions of the toe-hold-down bindings of the past. They are totally functional, grasping the elongated sole of the boot tightly so that the heel can be lifted. The idea is to eliminate fatigue while traversing long stretches of terrain. The lightweight nature of cross-country gear helps. Skis weigh about 3–4 pounds, boots not much more, bindings virtually nothing. Because the good cross-country skier is akin to a human furnace, no matter how cold the weather is, he dresses in light layers—nylon or poplin outer anorak, inner sweater, turtleneck shirt, net undershirt. Comfort dictates the selection of knickers and long socks. Many of the instructional pictures in this book were taken at temperatures of 10–15 degrees below zero, yet Art Tokle while demonstrating wore only lightweight clothing, albeit several layers of it. Cross-country skiers at speed are the embodiment of the physical principle of the conversion of energy into heat.

There seems to be a great deal of controversy over what sort of skis is proper for the new cross-country devotee—light and narrow racing skis, light and less narrow "light" touring skis, or the wider and slightly heavier general touring variety. The same conflict extends to boots; there are those that opt for starting out with racing skis coupled with the low-cut racing boot, others that back the low-cut boot and "light touring" ski, and still others that feel that the beginner should purchase the wider general touring ski, higher cut boot, and the kind of binding (Tempo) that grasps the heel as well as the toe but does not hold the heel down. There are, in fact, at least two dozen models of cross-country skis on the market, more than half a dozen types of bindings, and a rather large variety of poles, boots, waxes, and other accessories. With this plethora of gear available, it is easy to become confused—especially when poor advice is given by a shop salesman, the type who suggests light racing equipment for elderly people and beginners. Herewith, therefore, some recommendations—and the reasons for them.

Racing skis and boots are *not* for elderly people and beginners. They are too light, too easily breakable, and too narrow and therefore unstable for the person who has never been on skis before or whose bag is going to be distance touring. Light touring skis (slightly wider than the racing version) are ok for persons with some alpine skiing experience, especially if a great deal of the time is going to be spent on prepared tracks. For this category of skier, low-cut boots are a matter of choice; our recommendation is for the slightly higher touring variety, which gives more support and stability over uneven terrain, especially when one is trying to get the hang of the sport.

It is obvious that we are rather pragmatic about the whole thing. The aim should be comfort and enjoyment, rather than trying to keep up with the in-crowd. Of the rules of thumb in selecting equipment, the most important is to make a judgment on the kind of skiing you are planning, that is, how often, where, and the kind of skier you honestly think you are. Because, despite the emphasis given to lightweight racing and touring skis and boots by one school of thought, we honestly believe that the beginner—and the person who intends to do a lot of trail breaking on rough terrain—

should equip himself with wider touring skis, higher boots, and the Tempo style of binding. Our reasons: the more lateral stability, better balance, and sturdiness provided by this kind of outfit help the beginner learn more quickly. However, if fashion seems to be edging you away from common sense, this chart may help with your decision.

KIND OF SKIING

	Racing	Touring competition	General touring
SKIS	Racing	Racing Extra light touring	Light touring Touring
BINDING	Pin	Pin	Pin
BOOTS	Racing	Racing Light touring	Light touring Touring

CUSTOMARY TERRAIN

	Developed trails	Woods, trails, rolling hills	Rough, hilly, no track
SKIS	Light touring Extra light touring	Light touring Touring	Touring
BINDING	Pin	Pin, Tempo, or cable	Tempo or cable
BOOTS	Light touring Touring	Light touring Touring	Touring

Ski mountaineering, which is a high-altitude form of cross-country and involves climbing, traversing, and downhill skiing, is not listed in the chart, because its equipment is more specialized—involving the use of downhill skis with the "clou" type of binding (which can be used with a loose heel or latched down for downhill runs), alpine boots, and climbing skins.

Let's analyze the cross-country equipment you'll need:

SKIS: LEAVING NO LIGNOSTONE UNTURNED

The beginner, of course, has no frame of reference, but the alpine skier will find cross-country skis unfamiliar at first. They are narrow (50–70 millimeters) compared to alpine skis (Fig. 8), longer, with more curve in the shovel, and surprisingly strong for their light weight. There was a time, in calculating proper length of alpine skis, when one used the system of placing the ski heel on the floor, tip just reaching the cupped hand held outstretched above one's head. Now, with the trend toward shorter downhill skis, a formulation is made based on weight, height, and skiing ability in determining alpine ski length. In selecting cross-country skis, however, the length is still determined in the traditional way (Fig. 9). Cross-country skis are categorized into 3 general types (Fig. 10).

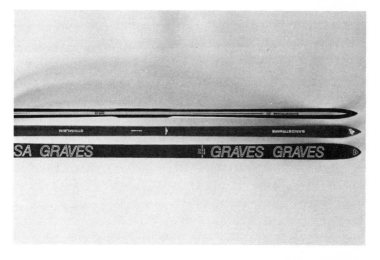

Figure 8. Light racing ski, top, compared with general touring and alpine skis beneath. Differences in weight and width are evident.

Figure 9. Checking correct ski length. Tip just reaches curved palm of hand held above head.

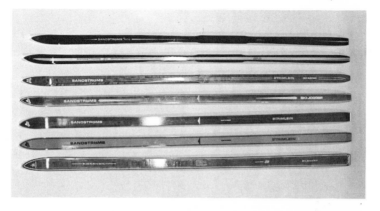

Figure 10. Range of cross-country skis varies from general touring, bottom, to light racing, top. Models suitable for you should be based on type of skiing, frequency of use, general ability.

GENERAL TOURING

About 70 millimeters (2¾ inches) at the tips, they are the widest of the cross-country skis and are most suitable for day-long backpacking trips on unbroken snow, where their stability and buoyancy are especially useful. Good to learn on and good for family use, they are recommended for those who do not ski regularly.

The best of the general touring skis are constructed of birch and spruce laminations with a top of beech and sole of hickory. Edges are lignostone—beechwood boiled in linseed oil and compressed to almost double its former density, making an incredibly hard and almost indestructible edge. General touring skis are usually provided with tail protectors to guard against delamination. Because of the kind of terrain they are designed for, the best skis of this type can stand up to an enormous amount of punishment. Weight: 5 to 5½ pounds; cost: $40–$50.

23

Another less expensive variation on the general touring ski is laminated birch with hickory edges. The hard hickory edge extends the lifetime of the ski and usually stays square. Weight: 4½ pounds; cost: $26–$35.

General touring skis also are made of laminated birch without edges and of solid birch. Nonlaminated skis are strong and inexpensive (about $20) but have a tendency to warp if not stored properly with a block between the bindings of the skis before they are strapped together.

LIGHT TOURING

These are about 60 millimeters (2⅜ inches) at the tips. Models vary in price based upon the number of spruce and birch laminations, which range from 22 to 28, and the kind of edges, of which lignostone is the best. Most suitable for touring on a prepared track, they are lighter than the general touring ski (about 3½ to 4 pounds). Many ski centers rent this kind of cross-country ski, which gives the would-be tourer an opportunity to determine whether they work for him. The most popular of the cross-country skis sold in the United States, they are priced from $30 to $40 (Fig. 11).

Figure. 11. Closeup of racing, top, and touring ski, bottom, shows difference in width.

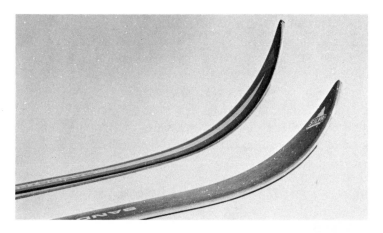

Figure 12. Deep curving shovel of racing ski, top, is graphically illustrated in comparison with light touring ski. Deep shovel helps racer "kick," but also makes ski more fragile.

RACING

Sleek and light, they are 50-millimeters wide at the tip. With a deep curving shovel, they are easily distinguishable from light touring skis (Fig. 12). One version, a sturdy spruce-birch laminate with hickory edges, is suitable for training young racers.

Besides general racing skis, there are special light competition skis laminated in construction with birch, spruce, and balsa wood making up the core. Edges are hickory or plastic. Some have built-in air channels to reduce weight. Generally they weigh less than 3 pounds and cost $43–$55.

SUMMARY

Purchase your skis based on the frequency of use and the type of terrain most frequently skied. Laminates with hick-

25

ory, lignostone, or plastic edges are the best of the wood skis. Pay up to $40. New fiberglass and metal competition skis also are on the market but can cost as much as $80. In selecting your skis, check the bottom camber (curvature in ski as seen in profile) by clicking the ski sole to sole with its mate. Skis should touch precisely from shovel to heel. Bottom camber is important—it helps provide utmost kick when springing from one ski to another while running.

BOOTS: THE OLD SOFT SHOE

The beginner, again, has no point of reference, but to the alpine skier accustomed to the rigid cementlike plastic structures used in downhill skiing, Nordic boots feel like carpet slippers (Fig. 13). Which is what they're supposed to be— soft, flexible, bendy things that vary in shape from a rela-

Figure 13. Cross-country boot is flexible and helps skier give the push that is so important in cross-country technique. Light racing boot here is combined with Rotefella binding and racing skis.

26

Figure 14. A bevy of cross-country boots from light low-cut racing to high-cut touring model.

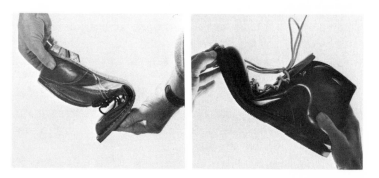

Figure 15. Low-cut racing boot, left, is as flexible as a carpet slipper compared to high-cut touring boot, right. But touring boot provides more ankle support. Note heel conformation on racing boot to prevent side slippage when skiing.

tively high ankle support to none at all. The latter, whose closest relatives are track shoes, are what cross-country racers wear. Between the two extremes are the boots for you (Fig. 14).

Uninsulated, with a slightly elongated leather or nylon sole to fit standard cross-country bindings, the boots should fit—with room for toes (in your ski socks)—like a well-made tennis sneaker. If they hurt, they are wrong, which is not usually the case with the alpine variety. The more comfortable they are, without being sloppy, the better.

There are 3 categories of cross-country boots:

27

TOURING

For touring in difficult terrain, breaking trail under all sorts of snow conditions, the high-cut touring boot is recommended. It can be single or double laced, but its main advantage is in the support it provides for comfortable skiing over long stretches of snow. Touring boots are usually used with Tempo or cable bindings; the combination provides maximum help to the skier when, for instance, he moves through such difficult snow conditions as breakable crust. Used with the wider, touring ski, the touring boot affords the beginner a way of learning the balance necessary for proper cross-country technique.

Touring boots are the heaviest of the cross-country boots (but not by much), and they are flexible enough for the kind of over-the-terrain work the typical Nordic tourer engages in.

LIGHT TOURING

Medium-cut, the light touring boot is the most popular of the boots used for general skiing. It comes in a variety of styles and colors; some are insulated and some women's models are fleece lined. Most practical for touring packed trails, the light touring boot is designed to be used with the pin-type binding, although on some models the heel is notched for the cable. Depending on price, soles are leather or composition.

RACING

Low-cut and lightest in weight, the racing boot is intended for those who compete, although the advanced cross-country skier can use it for touring on packed trails. Racing boots usually have composition soles and special heel shapes to reduce the tendency of snow to pile up under the heel. They are totally flexible, and styles range from basic black to the track shoe look.

SUMMARY

Boot prices range up to $35. In choosing boots, our guideline for equipment selection holds true. Your boots should match your skis and your intent. Avoid low-cut racing boots if you have no intention of competing but plan to spend your time outdoors touring. Insulated and fleece-lined boots are obviously designed to keep the feet warm, but they have a tendency to get damp from perspiration. Cold feet are not a cross-country problem; in motion, the body is so superheated that the feet remain warm even in below-zero temperatures.

BINDINGS: GETTING A TOEHOLD

Cross-country bindings are simplicity in themselves—the modern-day version of the toe-strap that held boots to the skis of the touring sportsmen of the last century. Some idea of the variety of bindings available is shown in the accompanying photographs (Fig. 16). *Cable* or *Tempo* bindings work with touring skis and boots; they have a releasable cable that fits around the heel of the boot to keep the boot from moving laterally.

All of the others, whether *pin* or *pinless* (pins are used to hold the boot toe to the binding), work on the same general principle—a spring clamp holds the toe of the boot in place and hooks under an adjustable ratchet (Fig. 17).

Figure 16. Gamut of bindings from touring and Tempo cable models, left, to pin and pinless Rotefella models with several versions of bail arrangements to grip boot sole tip.

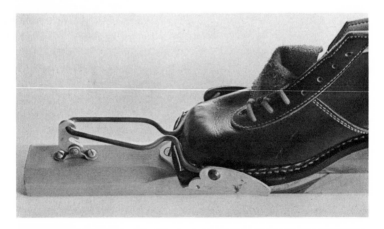

Figure 17. Light touring boot in binding. Note how bail holds down boot sole.

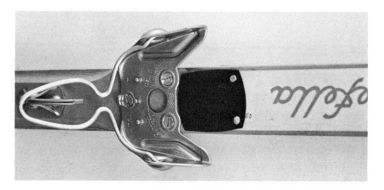

Figure 18. Popular 3-pin Rotefella binding. Pins fit into eyelets in boot sole to help grip boot and prevent wobble.

Most popular is the Rotefella, which uses 3 pins that fit into complementary holes in the sole tip (Fig. 18). More complicated is the Eie, which has no wire bail to hold the boot tip down but necessitates hardware on the boot. The average cost of bindings is $7–$10. Bindings should always be bought with some sort of heel retainer to keep the boot from wobbling sideways and to prevent snow from compacting under the boot.

POLES: BAMBOO IS BACK

Once all ski poles were made of bamboo until someone found a way of extruding aluminum and steel in thicknesses light enough to be practical. No one uses bamboo poles for alpine skiing anymore, but in cross-country they're still favored for their inexpensiveness and practicality. Select tonkin is the best among bamboos; it's springy yet strong. More expensive tonkin poles may be fiberglass wrapped for durability, and even more costly are total fiberglass and

31

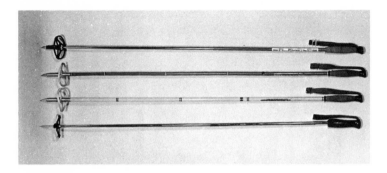

Figure 19. Poles may be fiberglass wrapped, top; tonkin, center; or lightweight metal, bottom.

metal (aluminum) poles, which are just finding their way to the market (Fig. 19).

SUMMARY

In choosing poles, again be guided by the frequency and type of your skiing. If you're bent on competition, fiberglass or metal poles are for you, because breakage is virtually nil, but they're more than twice as costly as good tonkin poles. Things to look for: cork handles to absorb perspiration (Fig. 20), an adjustable strap, and curved tips. If the tips aren't curved, they're not cross-country poles. The curved metal tip (see Fig. 21) facilitates pulling the poles out of the snow. Baskets are slightly larger than on the alpine variety. And they tend to be slightly longer than alpine poles, too, to provide more reach and push when skiing. Poles are an integral part of the technique of cross-country; they help provide the spring. To decide on size, here are 2 rules of thumb: (1) Deduct 13 inches from your height, or (2) with the pole handle on the floor, the *basket* should reach your armpit.

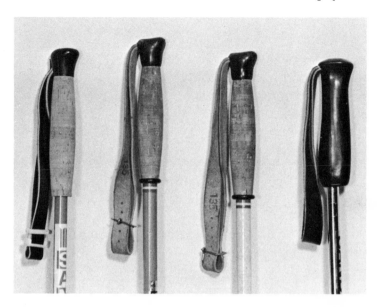

Figure 20. Pole handles should have adaptable strap. Strap on plastic handle can be adjusted at ski shop. Cork aids moisture absorption.

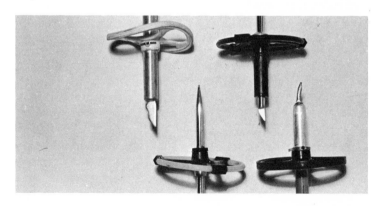

Figure 21. Typical cross-country pole tips are curved to aid removal from snow when skiing.

CLOTHING: KNICKERS AND KNEE SOCKS

Proper clothing for the well-dressed cross-country skier is dictated not by fashion but by good sense. Comfort is paramount, so on many trails it is possible to see some rather weird clothing combinations. However, again taking a cue from the Scandinavians, knickers and wool knee socks have become the accepted dress. With a bow toward the women, knickers are made in stretch nylon fabrics, sometimes trimmed at the knee with Norwegian patterns. Basic blues and bright reds are standard colors for knickers and anoraks; socks can be patterned or solid.

Some tips: Always dress in layers beginning with net underwear (its lacelike structure traps air and acts as an insulator), then turtleneck shirt, sweater or open-neck shirt, and light nylon or poplin anorak. A deep pocket across the front of the anorak is useful for carrying odds and ends such as stick waxes. A thin pair of cotton or silk

Figure 22. New light touring boot has built-in cuff to keep out snow.

socks under the wool knee socks helps keep the feet warm. The ability to remove a layer of clothing while running adds to comfort, but when at rest (during a lunch break on the trail, for instance), put the parka back on to keep from becoming chilled. In really cold, below-zero weather, normal alpine gloves can be worn. Lighter leather or cotton gloves are practical for warmer temperatures. When it's really warm (in the twenties), most cross-country skiers go bare-handed. Nylon gaiters help to keep deeper snow out of boot tops, although at least one brand of boots comes with built-in anklets that can be worn tucked in or out depending upon snow depth (Fig. 22).

ACCESSORIES

Certain extras are useful and recommended and can be purchased as one's commitment to cross-country skiing deepens. Here is a typical list:

Plastic or Aluminum Ski Tip   Useful on long cross-country trips if a ski breaks.

Waxes   Begin with a 3-wax kit containing basic blue, red, and green stick waxes, cork, and scraper. Waxing is essential, but the mystery that has surrounded it is not. A simplified waxing system appears later in this book.

Fanny Pack   For sunglasses, film, loose change, and other trail sundries.

Rucksack   Nylon or canvas, to hold dry socks and lunch plus all of the above, except for the fanny pack.

EQUIPMENT AND CLOTHING CHECKLIST

Typical Equipment Costs

Skis	$26–$ 45
Boots	25– 35
Bindings	7– 10
Poles	8– 25
Total	$66–$115

Typical Clothing Costs

Net undershirt	$ 3.50
Turtleneck shirt	7.00
Heavy sweater	15.00
Anorak	15.00
Knickers	15.00
Knee socks	6.00
Cotton socks	3.00
Gaiters	3.50
Total	$68.00

Typical Accessory Costs

Wax kit (3)	$ 5.50
Spare ski tip	2.50
Fanny pack	6.00
Rucksack	16.00
Extra waxes	4.00
Total	$34.00

3 Waxing

IT'S SIMPLER THAN YOU THINK

Alpine skiers who have been around awhile remember carrying wax packages and blocks of paraffin with them to make skis run faster on all types of snow. The object was (and is) to prevent the skis from sticking so as to turn easily while sliding downhill. Today, the recreational downhiller rarely uses wax. Except for wet, sticky snow, tough, smooth, polyethylene ski bottoms (Kofix or P-Tex) eliminate most sliding problems. Only alpine racers really wax. They have translated the art into a science, and among competitors one often hears an event (usually downhill) described as a "wax race," meaning that the snow was so slow and "grabby" that the proper wax made the difference between winning and losing. To the recreational skier, the edge between 69 and

70 mph is meaningless, but the racer translates that difference into hundredths of a second, which is often the gap between winners and losers.

In cross-country skiing, the art of waxing is related in intent but has a multiple purpose. Most important, it makes the skis go; they will not slide without wax. Cross-country skis have wood bottoms, which do not move or hold on snow very efficiently and, besides, absorb moisture. Cross-country touring, therefore, has a greater dependence on the art of waxing and has, in fact, revised it. It's supposed to be part of the sport's mystique, but from our point of view, too much has been made of this supposed black science. Only cross-country racers need to be precise about their waxing; the beginner can handle the problem in a much more simplified fashion.

Nordic skiers are required to glide across the countryside, climb hills, slide down them, and glide again. Wax is all-important in aiding the skier to perform all of these phases of touring with ease. Besides preventing moisture absorption and snow build-up, the correct surface wax allows the skier to glide freely, yet prevents him from slipping back when he's climbing. In proper Nordic technique, one ski has more weight on it as the skier pushes and springs from that ski to glide on the other one. Wax helps hold the weighted ski to the snow while allowing the unweighted ski to slide forward. Properly waxed, the good cross-country skier can travel at a good rate of speed literally straight up the reasonably inclined sections of a trail, yet he is not hindered when he slides down the other side.

Some cross-country skiers are wax nuts. They collect hard and soft waxes, cakes, and tubes with the avidity of pack rats. They own small propane burners to melt base wax in and are very precise about snow quality and air tempera-

Figure 23. Basic wax kit contains blue, red, and green stick waxes and scraper.

tures as well as the correct mixtures to use in any given weather situation. The beginner need not be so precise. A kit of 3 surface waxes plus burnishing cork and scraper costs about $5.50 and will suffice at the start to cover most eventualities (Fig. 23). More waxes can be acquired later as the need arises. To avoid confusion, since there are at least 5 major brands of wax on the market, most Nordic aficionados concentrate on one brand in order to learn the characteristics under varied snow conditions. In our case, without making recommendations one way or another, we use Swix for our simplified waxing system (Fig. 24).

To start with, a differentiation must be made between "base" waxes and "surface" waxes. Base waxes serve two functions: to impregnate the wood bottom of the ski to protect it from water absorption while at the same time helping it flex, and to provide a good gripping face for surface waxes, base wax *must* be used. The process of laying it in

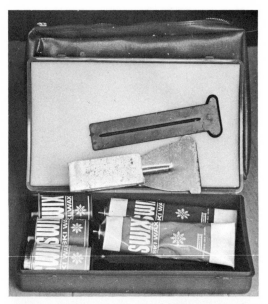

Figure 24. Touring pack, top, contains 3 stick waxes, 2 klisters, spreader, and scraper and is easily carried in skier's rucksack. Bottom, the whole wax works including base waxes in spray can and brush-on varieties, heater, and burner for melting in base and surface waxes.

once was considered a tedious chore, because the best way to do it involves the use of a torch to melt it into the wood surface. But to avoid the torch, there are now adequate substitute methods that are considerably easier on the nerves and the pocketbook.

Let's say you've brought your new skis home and they haven't had the base wax melted in at the store. Some ski shops will burn in the initial base wax as part of the selling price (or charge a minimal fee). Rather than get involved with the use of a torch the first time out, use a paint-on base, which is simpler to apply than household trim paint. It is really a pine tar–creosote combination that is laid on in overlapping strokes, then wiped down with a clean rag (Fig. 25). Several layers are recommended; they can easily be renewed during the skiing season. Two chair backs of equal height serve as a convenient rest for the skis, and the chairs themselves hold your waxing equipment out of the way until use.

Also on the market are spray-on base waxes. Application is done in the same way as spray paint. The can is not held too close to the ski (Fig. 26) so that the wax does not pile up. Nor is it held too far away; that would cause the wax to be dispelled in a broader area than just the ski. At the right height (try it first on a piece of scrap wood), use short overlapping strokes, then wipe in. Spray base is especially good for touch-ups during the season. If you feel up to using a torch, remember that the art of using it is all in the distance of the flame from the ski sole. Propane torches for base wax application come with a spreader head, but still, the great danger in the use of a torch is loss of concentration, which invariably leads to a charred ski bottom. For a short course in the use of a torch for melting in base wax, see the accompanying step-by-step illustration (Fig. 27).

Figure 25. Paint-on base wax technique. Brush from tip toward base in thirds, then wipe down with a clean rag. Use overlapping brush strokes.

Figure 26. Spraying base wax. Note distance of can from ski to avoid piling of wax, newspaper under ski to prevent wax from being dispelled elsewhere than on bottom. After spraying, wipe in.

Figure 27. Using a burner is tricky. Note distance of flame from ski bottom to prevent scorching ski sole. Wax is wiped on, then melted in, then smoothed out. Burners for use in waxing come with spreader head. Flame must be kept in constant motion.

Base waxing accomplished, you are ready to wax for skiing. But first:

SOMETHING ABOUT SNOW

From a distance, all snow, especially when it is recent, looks alike. But skiers know that snow can change from hour to hour in consistency and structure, causing very definite variations in the surface upon which one skis. The snow quality in sunny areas is different from that in the shade; wind, temperature, and relative newness all affect the surface and, therefore, your skiing.

As a general rule, without going into finer categories, snow can be divided into 3 types—*new, fine grained,* and *coarse grained.*

Figure 28. Cross-country expert Sverre Aamodt moves along in breakable crust.

New snow is just that—fresh while falling, or just after a fall. Crystals are large and rather loosely put together. After a short time, the fresh snow begins to pack and become fine grained, with the crystals changing shape and coming closer together. As the temperature warms without any new snow falling, snow tends to lose its delicate structure and pack into ice crystals of a *coarse-grained* nature. Old snow at warmer temperatures becomes crusty because the surface layer melts, then freezes together. Downhill skiers are familiar with the treacherous snow phenomenon known as "breakable crust," which can stop a skier in his tracks, usually resulting in an injury. Breakable crust is simply coarse-ground, hardened crystals over fine-grained snow. Cross-country skiers have no such fear—they simply trudge through the stuff (Fig. 28).

SOMETHING ABOUT TEMPERATURE

Below 32 degrees F, waxing is relatively simple; the lower the temperature, the harder the wax—light green, green, and blue. But when the mercury is at the freezing point, the temperature of the air and snow is not the same, and the criterion for waxing is based on the moisture content of the snow:

> *dry snow* falls away in flakes
> *moist snow* packs and holds together
> *wet snow* shows water on the surface

Use your gloved hand for testing; make a snowball and examine it.

The use of the simplified waxing chart at the end of this chapter becomes essential until one becomes proficient in snow and temperature judgment. One way of gaining proficiency is to keep a wax log; note time, temperature, snow type, and wax used each time you go out.

WAXING RIGHT

Hard waxes, mainly for temperatures below 32 degrees F, come in tins. Soft waxes, or "klisters," come in tubes. Whereas hard waxes are simple to apply, your typical klister has the consistency of molasses and no respect for the finicky. Improperly put away after using, it will spread outside its tube, with resultant mess. But klister is the only answer for wet, warm snow.

Skis must be dry before surface wax is spread. If you are using a hard wax, use short strokes over the entire surface of the sole, then burnish it with a cork, block, or the heel of your hand (see Fig. 29).

a.

b.

c.
Figure 29. Applying hard wax on the surface after base treatment. Use short strokes with the wax stick (*a*), then, after wax is applied to entire ski, burnish in with cork (*b*) or palm of hand (*c*). Then put skis outside so that wax can harden.

When using klister, apply indoors at room temperature. Squeeze an even bead on both sides of the center groove. Then use the spreader that comes with your wax kit (Fig. 30) to smooth the surface.

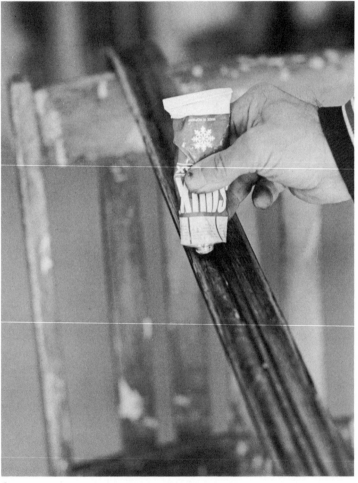

a.

b.
Figure 30. The art of applying klister is based on using control over the amount beaded on ski. Squeeze a light even bead on ski sole on both sides of groove, but not in it (*a*). Then smooth the surface with a spreader, holding it horizontally across the ski surface (*b*), then vertically to remove stray klister from groove (*c*).

51

c.

Some Waxing Tips

1. Always scrape or melt off previously used wax before applying the new surface wax (Fig. 31).
2. Wax for the coldest snow condition you think you'll find. Then, on the trail if you need to, you can apply a softer wax over the first wax if your skis aren't running properly. Remember, it takes several

Figure 31. After returning from a cross-country run, or before putting on new wax, remove wax completely with a scraper. Don't neglect groove.

hundred yards of skiing to "set" the wax. So don't make any judgments until you've gone a reasonable distance along the trail.

3. After waxing (it can be done indoors or out for hard wax), let your skis stand outside for a few minutes before you use them. Friction of corking warms the ski bottom. If the ski is placed in the snow, it will do a quick-melt job; then as the snow freezes again, it will form ice on the bottom of your ski. You will feel as if you are dragging an anchor along with your body. This is not fun.

4. In addition to your waxes, take along a scraper on the trail. You might just want to remove the old wax.

5. If you are taking klister along, put the tube in a plastic bag. It will save the inside of your rucksack, and your temper as well.

6. The rougher and thicker you apply the wax, the better it will be for uphill climbing, the poorer for gliding. How smooth the wax is applied requires some knowledge of the kind of terrain over which you'll be touring.

7. If you're slipping back on uphill portions and not getting enough "kick," try applying a softer wax to the heel, the shovel area, and the section under the boot.

Waxing for Long Tours

If you're planning a day trip on skis, the principle of waxing for the coldest snow you think you'll find (with the hardest wax) still applies. However, there are exceptions:

If you are moving from a lower altitude to a higher one, several hundred feet can make a great difference in snow consistency. You may need, for instance, a blue wax at the base elevation and green at the touring elevation; the higher the altitude, usually, the colder the snow. Since blue is softer than green, it will have to be scraped off before the harder green is applied. Rule: Always carry a scraper.

If you start early in the morning, the snow is bound to change as the day goes on—it will probably be colder, windier, warmer, etc., than when you started out. You will find rewaxing a necessity at some point during your tour. Rule: Carry a tour pack wax kit of 3 tins: green, blue, red. Red, applied thickly, will work as a substitute for klister if the temperature gets above 32 degrees during your tour.

And another rule. Don't wax at home if you are going to travel by car to your starting point. The temperature, weather, and snow conditions are bound to be different. Wax on the spot, even if you have to do it outside.

WAXING FOR RACERS

While the principles used in waxing are essentially the same, there are certain basic differences between the methods used by the touring skier, especially if he is inexperienced, and those practiced by the cross-country racer. For one thing, the racer wants his skis to be able to move quickly across the snow, and he has the technique to accomplish this. So he waxes "slick"—for as little friction as possible between ski and snow. Despite the fact that his skis are slippery, he still has the ability to march uphill without sliding backward, as opposed to the recreational tourer who needs a stickier wax to help him up grades. The racer accomplishes this by using the hardest wax possible for the day as a base coat, then shining that and other waxes in. The recreational skier must go to a slightly softer wax that will provide more gripping surface on uphill portions.

A SIMPLIFIED WAXING CHART

HARD WAX

Consistency	Color	Snow Type	Temperature, °F
Hardest	Light green	Cold, dry	Below 0° F.
Hard	Green	Dry, powdery, hard, old	10°–25° or colder
Less hard	Blue	Hardpack or frozen granular	20°–32°
Softer	Red	Wet	32°–40°
Soft	Violet	Old	32° and up
Softest	Yellow	Cloggy, wet, new	32° and up
Wax binder	Orange	Helps hold wax better on hard, cold snow	

KLISTERS

Consistency	Color	Snow Type	Temperature, °F
Least soft	Blue	Crusty, icy	20°–32°
Softer	Violet	Moist to wet, old, granulated	32°
Soft	Red	New, wet	32° and up
Softest	Special yellow	New, very wet	Above 32°

SPECIAL WAXES

Consistency	Color	Use
Paraffin	Milky	For speed on long downhill sections in temperatures above 32° F.

56

Racers are incredibly careful with torches when heating in tar for waterproofing. Their skis—lighter and weaker than touring skis—are severely affected by too much heat. Although every racer has his own formula for waxing, some general rules are recommended:

Scrape immediately after heating in the tar base, then follow by waxing with a base wax, *if* the day is cold and the snow likewise. Base waxes for racers are used only if the snow is likely to be abrasive; otherwise begin with the hardest layer of surface wax for the day, followed by thin layers for the varied conditions likely to be encountered along the course.

Soft waxes provide more "bite" than hard waxes, but they should not be used in subfreezing temperatures, because they will freeze and prevent good forward glide.

For average tracks, wax should be rubbed out to a very smooth finish; time should be taken to do this. The only exception is for hard-packed snow, in which case the top layer should be left slightly uneven.

Use a cork for polishing heated-in surface waxes to prevent the possibility of flaking during the run.

4 The Technique of Cross-Country Skiing

LIKE A LEOPARD IN CARPET SLIPPERS

Among the clichés that one hears among some alpine ski instructors is the phrase "If you can walk, you can ski." While at least one book has been written using this idea as its theme, we think this is a patently false concept for downhill beginners because it doesn't take into account the fact that alpine skiing has very little to do with walking. Cross-country skiing *does,* and therein lies the difference in learning the two allied sports.

To accomplish the art of alpine skiing reasonably well, the skier has a lot of *unlearning* to do, mainly because he is dealing with his natural reaction to gravity on a rather steep inclined surface that is usually bumpy, icy, and filled with other skiers. At the same time, he must somehow overcome many fears—fear of going too fast, of not being in control, of collision with an inanimate object, such as a tree, or an animate object, such as another skier.

Making turns that take you where you want to go in alpine skiing takes a large amount of coordination when done smoothly. Good parallel turns at speed are not easy to accomplish, and there are many recreational skiers who remain at one learning plateau or another and never really go any further, because to be a good downhill skier one needs a great deal of constant effort on the mountain. Most recreational skiers simply do not ski often enough to become very advanced in their ability. This is not to say that they don't have fun at their own level of accomplishment. They do have occasional superb days on the mountain when conditions are just right, but when they are not, despite the brave smiles, their attempts to ski mark a fine line between enjoyment and masochism.

What we are saying, as alpine skiers ourselves, is that becoming a good downhill skier is not easy, but becoming a competent cross-country skier is. In fact, one morning's instruction in Nordic technique is enough to send anyone who has never been on skis before, provided he is reasonably well coordinated, on his way across lots. One morning's instruction in alpine skiing guarantees a free ride on the bunny tow and the dictum to stay away from anything more serious than the "nursery" slopes. The cross-country instructor knows he can turn his pupils loose with impunity; they are not in any danger when they take off, because the possibility of damaging oneself, other than having sore muscles from overdoing it the first day, is almost unheard of.

Figure 32. In full stride, Sverre Aamodt chugs up a slight incline with perfect technique.

In any case, you have your new skis, your wax kit, poles, boots, and clothing, and you're ready to go. The night before you head for the trails, you can get the feel of cross-country skiing indoors with a pair of leather-soled slippers of the "flip-flop" variety and a smooth carpet. Starting with your feet together, push with the toes of the left foot so that you slide flat-soled with the right. Then switch; lift the heel of the right foot, push, and slide the left foot forward. On snow, cross-country skiing is the logical extension of these motions—moves that are similar to the steps in ice skating, except that in touring the push is straight ahead instead of at an angle to your forward path. (You can skate on skis, too, not only ahead, but as a means of turning, as we shall see.)

Poles are used in this push-and-glide technique to help get that added drive. The poles, in the most frequently used technique, are used diagonally—like arm-swinging when you walk. In fact, cross-country technique is simply walking speedily on snow (Fig. 32).

To push and glide, you'll find, takes balance—you glide with one leg on one ski at a time. One way of developing good balance is to practice on terrain that is flat, but not hard packed, without using poles to get the feel of gliding on each ski. Knees are bent, body slightly curled and centered. You spring from one ski to another like a leopard in carpet slippers (Fig. 33).

Climbing is easy too. With the proper wax, you can climb nonsteep inclines straight ahead, remembering only to take shorter strides and not lean forward too much. Steeper terrain is handled with the herringbone, or sidestep, or forward-climbing traverse and kick turn (Fig. 34).

Running down, knees are bent, body in a kind of forward-tilting question mark. Practice downhill running on an easy

Figure 33. Balance exercises. Left, Per Soerlie demonstrates correct way to practice balance. Leg is high, with ski tip tilted down. Practice on a slight incline, alternating skis. Right, beginner is afraid to raise ski higher, keeps tip pointed up awkwardly which will throw her backward and cause a fall.

grade with a natural runout so that the skis will come to a stop by themselves. Stopping and braking is accomplished with a snowplow, riding one's poles, or by grabbing the

Figure 34. The herringbone. Beginners are practicing without poles to attain feel of skis.

nearest tree, a technique that is not frowned upon among cross-country tourers.

There are several turn variations—kick turn and stepping

around on the flat, and for inclines, snowplow, half-stem, and skating turns.

The cross-country skier has ways to rest, too, while skiing. Double poling—the use of both poles together to push both skis in to a glide—is one way of easing effort on the trail.

Actually, when you're learning, almost anything goes in cross-country. The sport is dedicated to freedom, and the object is not to clench your teeth and try to ski like the racers do, but simply to move along a trail at a pace that you set yourself. The point is to be out there exploring the winter world of forest and field, making your own tracks or enjoying a day's tour with friends sparked by an outdoor lunch, warmed by a fire dug deep into the snow and a good red wine.

While we realize that you can't ski with this book in your hand, we suggest that you study the pictures and text on the following pages as a method of familiarizing yourself with the basic maneuvers, or as a way of correcting the errors you have made during the day. The photos represent a pictorial short course in cross-country technique and are followed by some examples of the Nordic art as practiced by several of America's top Olympians.

THE BASICS OF CROSS-COUNTRY SKIING

BODY POSITION

In a standing position, the skier is always relaxed, knees slightly bent, head erect, and eyes forward. A common fault among beginning skiers is this last; eyes are on the skis rather than on the trail. Result—the head is tilted down with an attendant effect on the skier's technique. The good cross-country skier is always aware of the track ahead, knowing that the skis will take care of themselves. Poles are in the ready position; arms are parallel to the ground (see Fig. 35).

Figure 35. Basic body position of the skier at rest. Knees are slightly bent, upper body tilted slightly forward, head up.

USE OF POLES

In cross-country skiing, poles are an integral part of body movements, providing the extra push to enable the skier to glide either on one ski, as in the diagonal stride, or on both, as in "double poling."

To hold poles properly, place hands through the strap from *underneath,* then grasp the pole handle, letting both sides of the strap ride across the palm between thumb and index finger. The grasp should be firm but relaxed; the poles are not crutches and cannot be expected to do all of the work for you (Fig. 36).

Figure 36. Holding the pole. Place hands through strap from underneath; grasp pole handle. Both sides of the strap run smoothly across the palm.

The straps should be adjusted so that they loosely hold the hand against the grip. If they are too tight, the hands will get tired. When running, whether in single pole (diagonal) or double pole, remember to let them hang loosely as they are thrust back (as the ski passes the planted pole), held only by thumb and forefinger. To do otherwise—grasping the pole tightly to keep the tip up behind you—is another common beginner's fault and also results in weary arms.

TURNING ON THE FLAT

You are ready to take your first steps on skis, which is as good a time as any to learn how to change direction. Make sure you have picked level terrain on which to practice. Preferably the snow should not be hard packed, but with enough powder to keep you from slipping.

The Step Turn It's the most simple method of changing direction, but it is useful only when the terrain is level. Practice first without poles to get the feel and balance of your skis. Let's assume you want to turn to the right. Start with skis together in the basic body position. Then lift the right ski at a slight angle, tip brushing the snow, heel up, and place it in the snow. Transfer your weight to that ski and bring the other one next to it. Keep repeating the maneuver until you have turned full circle. Then, for practice, try the step turn in the other direction (Fig. 37).

With poles it's actually simpler, because placement of the pole helps you transfer your weight more easily. With poles, you can do the step turn on more of an incline. The pole is placed in the snow midway between the binding and tip in the direction you wish to turn. Your weight is shifted,

a.
Figure 37. Step turn without poles. Begin with basic position (*a*).
Then lift ski at a slight angle (*b*), and place it in the snow.
Then (*c*) bring other ski next to it. Remember to keep ski tip down
to aid balance.

69

b.

c.

and the other ski (and pole) is brought up to it and so on into another full circle (Fig. 38).

a.
Figure 38. Step turn with poles (*a–e*). The technique is the same, except that pole use helps you move with more balance and, therefore, speed.

72

b.

c.

d.

e.

Remember to keep your knees slightly bent. If you lift the heel more than the tip, you will automatically keep your weight forward and prevent losing your balance with a resultant fall backward. Bring the skis together before you start another step.

The Kick Turn   A smooth kick turn is a necessary part of
the repertoire of the person who intends to do much cross-
country touring, because it's the simplest method of changing
direction in a standing position on a slope. Tourers use
it when coming to the end of a traverse, either climbing or
going downhill. While the kick turn once was one of those
maneuvers that all alpine skiers learned, very few now take
the trouble to accomplish it. With the bulky held-down
boot of downhill gear, one must be rather limber to do it
well. Not so for the cross-country type, who has the advantage of a free heel and light, flexible skis.

The kick turn should be done in one fluid movement
(Fig. 39). Assuming that you want to reverse your direction
to the left, place your right ski pole near the outside tip of
your right ski and your left ski pole near the tail of the left

a.
Figure 39.   Kick turn. Turning to the left, place right pole near
outside tip of right ski and left pole near tail of other ski (*a*).

77

b.
Balance yourself on both poles and lift left ski so that tail is near tip of right ski and tip is angled across your left shoulder (b).

c.
Place ski in snow (c)

d.
and step around (*d*). Practice so that you can do it in one fluid motion.

ski. Now, using the poles for balance, lift your left ski so that the tail of the ski is in the snow near the inside tip of your right ski and let its weight carry it down toward the direction you wish to turn. Then, simply step around with the other ski, still using your poles for balance. You are now facing in the opposite direction from which you started.

Practice on the level first, then on an incline. On a steeper slope, leaning back against the poles slightly helps make the turn easier.

WALKING AND GLIDING

The Old Soft Shoe Shuffle   Turns on a flat surface help you get the feel of your skis and some idea of how much balance is required to keep them flat on the snow. Now you can begin to learn the rudiments of cross-country running. Like swimming, for instance, which requires consistent, smooth, equal movements that rarely vary, cross-country skiing done well becomes part of one's kinetic memory. Once it is well learned, it is always there. Refinement, once you have gotten past the basics, means only the lengthening of stride, the ability to push harder and glide longer, and the development of stamina.

Begin without poles in the old soft shoe shuffle. We've said that if you can walk, you can ski. So, without poles, just shuffle along as if you were walking, alternating arm swings. Don't attempt to spring from one ski to the other, but rather concentrate on maintaining balance while moving, keeping the body relaxed and the head up, your eyes looking forward. Try to unweight one ski slightly and slide on the other. Then reverse skis (see Fig. 40).

a.
Figure 40. Stride without poles. A way of getting used to your skis is simply to walk on them without using poles to push. First concentrate on shuffling along (*a*).

b.

c.

Then try pushing with one ski and gliding with the other (*b* and *c*). The technique is similar to making a scooter move. Keep your body square to the skis and swing your arms.

Keep your knees bent, press one ski down, and glide. Your body should be square to the skis, your arms swinging almost up to shoulder level. Try not to sway from side to side. Practice on level terrain for a short run of 100 yards or so, then step turn around and come back to the starting point. Aim for smoothness.

DOUBLE POLING

Double poling is a way of resting while running, as a change from the diagonal stride. Changing from one method to the other will be discussed later. Double poling is useful on slight declines to maintain speed, yet it allows the skier to relax.

Keeping the skis parallel, push with both poles simultaneously and glide, letting the poles trail behind you. Then plant the poles forward again and push as the skis glide past them (see Fig. 41).

Figure 41. Double poling (*a–c*). Keep skis slightly apart, push down and back with your poles, and slide until momentum diminishes. Push again.

a.

b.

c.

DIAGONAL POLING

The Basic Cross-Country Stride   Once you have experienced the arm-swinging feeling of the old soft shoe shuffle with the push attained from bending the toes of your boots while letting the skis slide, skiing with poles will come naturally (see Fig. 42).

a.

b.
Figure 42. Diagonal stride with poles (*a–c*). The basic running technique is simply a matter of rhythmically pushing and gliding, using poles to attain extra push in an arm-swinging motion. Note that pole is placed in front and to the side of ski to achieve a pendulumlike effect that aids glide on opposite ski.

c.

Again the technique resembles walking, but as if you were reaching out with two canes to help you move along faster. Drive in the diagonal stride comes from the push generated by the bended knee of the weighted ski. The other ski is behind you, ready to come forward and be weighted as you push with the pole on the weighted side. There is a constant right-left rhythm that translates itself into a longer glide and greater push as you learn to spring off your toes from one ski to the other—always deriving power from your bent knees. Arms and legs are opposed. Study the sequence photos (Figs. 42 and 43) and notice that there is little sideways movement, no bobbing of the head and bending at the waist.

As you become more practiced in the basic stride, you'll find yourself pressing farther back with your "kick" and leaning somewhat more forward as you stretch into your glide. But try to keep the heel of the unweighted ski down—raising it too high is wasted motion (Fig. 43).

Poles are planted at the sides of the skis near the tips as you drive "past" them. Keep your hands parallel to the skis and try not to swivel them across your chest, which will rock you from side to side and is also wasted effort. Initially, level terrain with a good packed snow surface is best for practice.

a.
Figure 43. Diagonal stride at speed (*a–d*). Some points to note: Body is always kept level and does not swing from side to side. This is controlled by placement of hands and by reaching poles in front

b.
of and slightly outside of where the ski will be. Pole pushes as ski slides alongside pole. Ski tips are always tilted down. As you gain proficiency, reach out further with your poles and push harder with your skis so that you will, in effect, spring smoothly from one ski to the other.

91

c.

d.

Skiing Uphill

The cross-country track and the tourer's route are never precisely level. No skier would want them to be, because a great deal of the enjoyment of cross-country skiing is found in the handling of mixed terrain. A golf course that anyone can walk with ease in the summer is transformed by snow into a varied mixture of hills and gullies and makes surprisingly good cross-country territory. Exploring on your skis in winter will most likely take you uphill, and you should be able to engage slopes smoothly even though doing it properly may seem like punishment at first. Climbing at a regular pace, however, is the best stamina- and strength-building exercise you can find. Based on relative steepness, there are several methods of climbing, and you should be able to use them all.

Straight Uphill Climbing   For lighter inclines, use the diagonal stride. The push-and-glide sequence is shorter, and while the temptation is to bend from the waist, don't do it, but do keep the body weight forward. The experienced skier and the racer virtually sprint uphill, taking quick, short steps because they know they can double pole or rest in the downhill glide on the other side. Racers take steep uphill portions on a course as if they were flat. Racers, however, practice this as part of their running technique. The recreational skier may eventually achieve this ability, but most often he climbs with the use of one of the oldest maneuvers in skiing (see Fig. 44).

The Herringbone   On steeper portions of the trail or on open slopes, going straight up is accomplished with the use

94

Figure 44. Uphill running. Steps are shorter and quicker, almost as if you were hustling up the grade. Don't bend from the waist, but keep your head up.

Figure 45. Herringbone. For climbing steeper slopes. The skis are in a V. Press the inside edges down to achive control. The steeper the slope, the wider the V. Poles are never planted forward of the ski binding.

of the herringbone, which is simply a series of V's up the grade (see Fig. 45). Skis are spread at the tips (but not too wide—width of spread is dependent upon degree of slope) and, again using opposite arms and legs, plant the pole toward the tail of one ski and push forward onto the inside edge of the other. With that ski weighted on its inside edge, push with ski and pole, and lift the other ski into the opposite side of the V. There is a point of steepness where the herringbone is no longer suitable for climbing. It is also difficult to use on hard-packed ("concrete") snow surfaces, where new powder has been scraped clean, or on icy areas. Now the side step becomes more useful.

The Side Step   The side step is a simple but slow way of climbing steep slopes. It is part of the tourer's repertoire and allows him not only to climb, but to safely negotiate slopes that he cannot traverse or run downhill. It is rarely if ever used on a packed cross-country track (Fig. 46).

a.

Figure 46.   Sidestep (*a–c*). Like climbing stairs sideways. Use the poles and skis together rhythmically and remember to keep the tips across the hill. Use pressure on the uphill edges of your skis so that the skis cut into the snow on the slope.

b.

c.

With poles approximately in line with the boots and skis parallel, begin by planting the upper pole a couple of feet above your body. Push down on that pole and lift your uphill ski to it. Then bring your downhill ski up so that your skis are parallel again. On steep slopes, remember that you must edge into the hill with the outside edge of your uphill ski and the inside edge of your downhill ski. The skis *must* be straight across the slope. If the tips tilt downhill, you will begin sliding forward and down, and if they are pointed slightly uphill, you will begin sliding backward. Side stepping down a slope is the reverse of this procedure. Most important is the use of edges, especially when side stepping down a slope, because the skis are actually cutting into the slope rather than riding on the surface. In raising the skis, keep the tips down slightly, which will help you keep your weight forward—a salient point in all maneuvers in cross-country skiing.

Traversing Uphill For gradual climbs up untracked, steeper slopes, especially where you are trying to gain altitude, the traverse is best and, in fact, is another one of the tools used by the high-mountain tourer. It may be coupled with a kick turn when you reach the outer limit of the slope and wish to turn around and continue up it (Fig. 47).

Traversing uphill is more related to the elementary soft shoe shuffle than to the diagonal stride used on the packed track. Arms and legs are used oppositely in a kind of inclined trudge step that involves very little glide. The steeper the slope, the more use of the edges is needed. Poles are used not only for balance, but to give you the extra push you need to keep going and prevent tiredness. The angle at which you climb across the slope need not be steep; the flatter the angle, the more traverses you will have to make

a.

b.

Figure 47. Uphill traverse (*a–c*). Simply a trudge along a gradient. Use poles and skis as in the diagonal technique, but without the glide.

99

c.

to get to the top. The steeper the angle, obviously, the fewer traverses you make. Judgment of this is based on how well you are holding in the snow and its depth and consistency. Traverse tracks across a slope look like a switchback from afar.

SKIING DOWNHILL

On a prepared track, downhill gradients are the opportunity for resting while moving. For the beginner, there is a certain amount of fear involved in facing the first downhill run—but once the technique of doing it comfortably is accomplished, fear disappears and is replaced by confidence. Direct downhill running (Fig. 48) can be done on slopes as well as prepared tracks. When touring, some cross-country skiers prefer long gentle downhill traverses across open slopes. The angle of descent is governed by the depth and consistency of the snow, as well as the speed you feel you can handle easily.

a.

b.

Figure 48. Downhill running. From starting position (*a*) with poles placed at ski sides to hold you in place, sink into crouch (*b, c*) with your head up, derriere down, legs comfortably apart so that you are balanced on your skis. Pole tips are up.

101

c.
Body position can be likened to a reversed question mark. Skis should be kept flat.

Downhill Running   Start by practicing on a gentle slope with a runout that will bring you to a gradual stop. At the top of the slope, hold yourself in position with the poles placed in front of you forward and to the sides of the ski tips, arms in a continuous line with the poles. The skis should be comfortably apart so that you are well balanced on them. Your body is slightly crouched. Your head is up so that you do not bend forward from the waist. Knees are bent slightly; they act as shock absorbers as you ride your skis over bumps. Now, bring your weight forward and slide through your poles, moving the baskets up behind you. Your hands, grasping the pole handles, are together as you drop into the crouch and slide downhill.

Some tips on downhill running:

1. Don't sit too far back. Pressure on the tips of your skis is what controls the speed. The more you press forward with your knees, the more control you have. Sitting backward will lead to a backward fall. However, if you feel out of control, this is the safest and most pleasant way to fall; your stern, dragging through the snow, will apply the braking power to bring you to a snowy halt. Falling over the tips of the skis, while not dangerous with cross-country gear, will give you an instant spread eagle plus a very wet and embarrassed face.

2. Practice your crouch first without poles, then with them, on slopes that increase in steepness.

3. Make a bridge by inserting two poles in the snow and another across the handles, and try to run under it.

4. Keep a flat ski. Don't edge.

5. Balance is everything. One way to ensure balance is to keep your skis *comfortably* apart as you ride them downhill—too far apart and the inside edges will dig in; too close together and balance, at least for beginners, becomes more difficult (Fig. 49).

6. In heavier, unpacked, or deeper snow, sit back more than you normally would to bring the ski tips up so that they plane over the snow surface; otherwise the tips will tend to dig in and you will do a header into the snow.

7. The skis should run smoothly in colder weather. However, if the weather is warm and the snow sticky and you foresee a large amount of downhill running on the trail, carry a small block of paraffin, which can be applied quickly over the surface wax.

Figure 49. Downhill running. Another view.

104

Downhill Traverse   Your position is more like the traverse stance of the alpine skier—skis closer together, uphill edges cutting into the hill. You are more upright than you would be while running straight downhill. Your upper body leans slightly outward to compensate for the pull of gravity, which tends to make you want to lean into the hill. But if you do, your skis will slide away from under you and you will fall. Your pole baskets are again behind you but closer to the snow than in the straight downhill running position. At the end of your traverse, do a kick turn to take you into a new traverse in the other direction.

BRAKING

"How do I stop?" Good question—and the one most frequently shrieked by beginners as they come whizzing past their instructor and finally come to a rest by sitting down in the snow. There are better methods of slowing down and coming to a halt, although, as we've mentioned, anything goes in cross-country, including grabbing the nearest birch tree. Here are some of the more acceptable techniques:

Snowplow   The snowplow, almost ruled out of alpine skiing, is the cross-country skier's most popular method of staying in control on downhill tracks and slopes. It's also used for turning. The snowplow is an inverted V formed by the skis and allows you to exert sufficient pressure to keep the skis from running away with you (Fig. 50).

Start in the same position used for basic downhill running, except, with the pole tips placed in front of the skis to keep you from sliding forward, close the ski tips so that there is about a hand's breadth between them, and spread the tails of the skis so that you can comfortably press them outward.

Figure 50. Snowplow position. The snowplow is a herringbone in reverse—an inverted V. Tips are a hand's breadth apart. Control the skis by pressing inward on the inside edges.

Then slide forward between your poles, with the pole baskets again behind you. Now press down and out on the *inside* edges of your skis, and you will find that you can easily control your speed. To stop, press down *hard* on the inside edges while pressing the tails out (Fig. 51). To turn, exert more pressure on the inside edge of one ski than on the other and you will turn in that direction (Fig. 52).

Some tips: Your ski tips should always be the same hand's breadth apart, no matter how wide the tails are spread. Widening the tail spread with stronger pressure helps on steeper terrain, although this must be carefully gauged on the typical cross-country track. However, it works on open slopes. Don't forget to bend the knees and keep your weight pressed slightly forward. Hands should be down at belt level.

a.
Figure 51. Snowplow stop (*a–c*). By pressing down and out on the skis, you come to a stop. Concentrate on keeping tips of skis apart, constant pressure on inside edges. This will prevent tips from crossing. Knees are bent and pressed slightly forward, body in a slight crouch.

b.

c.

a.

b.
Figure 52. Snowplow turn. Weighting the inside edge of one ski more than the other (*a*) will cause you to turn in the direction of the weighted ski (*b*). Practice linked snowplow turns. Simply shift weight from one ski to the other (*c*).

110

c.

A slight outward lean with your shoulders in the direction you are turning helps to steer the turn.

Half Stem   In the half stem, one ski is kept straight and the other pressed out at an angle to the straight ski. The body position is the same as in the snowplow. Pressing on the inside edge of the angled ski will slow you down, although it may not bring you to a complete halt. The half stem is a good braking maneuver on inclines where you want to control your speed but not slow down as much as you would be slowed by the snowplow. Again, keep the ski tips about a hand's breadth apart.

The half stem is also used for turning. Put the ski out at an angle, then shift your weight to it. You will turn in the direction it is pointing. Then bring the other ski alongside it. Practice this on an open slope, in both directions. Make sure the slope is packed during your first tries at the half stem before you use it in deeper snow.

Braking with Poles　In the old days, skiers carried one pole. It had only one function—to keep the skier from traveling too fast downhill. The pole was used as a brake, either at the side, the skier pressing its lower end down into the snow to slow his progress, or actually sitting on it to weight the lower end into the snow.

No self-respecting alpine skier would use this technique today—and actually has no need to, because with the control he achieves through his held-down heel, he can stop efficiently in several different ways. The cross-country skier, however, with his lifting heel, does not have this much control and, therefore, thinks nothing of reverting to this nineteenth-century technique when he has to. It's strictly one for the tourer, best used on steep terrain when he wants to come straight down. The racer, of course, has no need for it, because his object is speed. And, of course, it's never used on prepared tracks by the recreational skier, because it digs up the trail.

Figure 53.　Braking. This technique is as ancient as the art of skiing and began when skiers carried one long pole to be used only when they needed to slow down or stop.

Try it for fun. Place both poles at your side, one hand on the handles, the other down low enough to press the baskets into the snow—and take off (Fig. 53).

ANOTHER TURN

We've illustrated the snowplow and half stem turns. One other method of turning—most used on trails to change directions yet maintain speed—is the moving step turn, or skating turn. It completes the repertoire of turns the recreational skier should know and be able to accomplish and is very much related to the way an ice skater changes direction (Fig. 54).

While in the diagonal stride, simply point one ski in the direction you want to go; and before you place it down,

a.
Figure 54. The skating turn. Also known as the moving step turn. Coming out of the diagonal stride, point one ski in the direction you want to go (*a*).

113

b.
Place the weight on that ski (*b*).

c.
Move off in the new direction (*c*).

114

push off with the opposite ski, glide on the angled ski in the new direction, and bring the other ski up to it, then continue with your diagonal movement down the track.

This turn is most applicable when trying to maintain speed when you come to turns in the trail.

THE CHANGE-UP

We've discussed diagonal (or single-pole) running and the double-pole technique as a change of pace. When gliding along a trail, it's more efficient to go from one to the other without losing rhythm. The change-up is simple to do. When one pole is forward in your diagonal stride, bring the other one (and its ski) up parallel, and then, using both poles to push, you can literally leap forward and glide on both skis (Fig. 55). Don't forget to trail the poles behind you at the end of the sequence, letting them rest in the half-closed palms of your hands, before you swing them forward again. Racers achieve tremendous momentum with the double-pole technique—leaning very far forward and literally reaching

a.
Figure 55. Change-up. A useful technique for switching from the diagonal stride to double pole and vice versa.

115

b.
Coming out of a diagonal stride (*a*), with one ski forward, bring the other ski up to it (*b*).

c.
Reach forward with both poles (*c*), and press back. You are now double poling.

116

out as far as they can with the poles before driving the skis ahead. But it's unnecessary for the recreational skier.

SOME TIPS TO MAKE YOU BETTER THAN YOU ARE

When you've reached the point where you can accomplish all of the maneuvers of cross-country skiing and have been able to develop reasonable rhythm on the trail as well as handle varied terrain with good control, there are some refinements that may help you ski better. Smoothness in cross-country aids in the building of stamina and allows you to ski longer distances without becoming too tired.

The "Kick"   Concentrate on keeping the unweighted "rear" ski low. Raising it too high adds to the strain on the leg muscles, besides being awkward (Fig. 56).

Bobbing   A common fault is bobbing the head on each stride. Try to keep your head level and let your body do the work. Look ahead.

Power   You'll get more power in your running if you keep your body (and your weight) forward. A smooth spring and drive come from use of the momentum carried by that forward leg as it comes back. The knees are like springs, too, and aid in the kick forward. (You wouldn't jog with stiff legs, would you?)

Fluid Motion   All of you works together in cross-country skiing. Arms and poles, legs, toes, and skis. Like a leopard in carpet slippers.

Figure 56. The kick. Power of a good kick is shown by Art Tokle as he extends himself on the trail. Note drive that is generated by long reach forward, top. As he glides, bottom, tail of "kicking" ski is kept low, pole is parallel with ski. Right leg is almost fully extended and right pole is ready to dig in to begin kick with left ski.

A LOOK AT THE OLYMPIANS

When you've reached Olympic status as a racer, it's assumed that you've been able to put together all the techniques we've discussed, after years of competition and constant practice, add your own refinements, and be able to take the trail with the world's best. Our readers may not have this sort of ambition, but a careful perusal of the accompanying photos of members of the U.S. Cross-Country Team in action at the Olympic Winter Games in Sapporo, Japan, may help you iron out some of the problems encountered in your own cross-country running (Fig. 57).

a.

Figure 57. Olympians in action. Photographed during 1972 Olympic Winter Games in Sapporo, Japan. American Olympic cross-country team members show slight personal variations in style. Mike Gallagher's form (*a*) is almost perfect although it could be

119

b.

argued that the weight of his upper body is more forward than necessary and the back pole is not being carried in a relaxed manner. The photo, however, signifies speed; Gallagher's powerful kick is carrying him forward at a rapid rate.

Tim Caldwell (b) has his body weight over his forward leg and does not kick high as he speeds along Olympic track. Note relaxed manner in which his pole trails. Rather than gripping it tightly, he simply guides it with his fingers. Poles and opposite legs are parallel.

120

c.

Barbara Britch (*c*) is all determination during women's cross-country competition. She is intent on track ahead, displays obvious power. American cross-country women skiers are up and coming in events that were once the sole property of Russian and Scandinavian women (Jim Balfanz photos).

5 Conditioning

PREPARING YOURSELF
FOR CROSS-COUNTRY SKIING

Throughout this book we've used the word "stamina" to describe the difference between the casual cross-country skier and the hard-nosed racing type, whether he be involved in head-to-head competition on the typical cross-country course or in the less technically demanding long-distance touring races that have become so popular in many parts of the country.

Stamina, as we see it, does not necessarily require great muscular strength, but rather it might be defined as the pushing back of the outer limits of exhaustion. To put it in the recreational skier's terms, a long tour is not much fun if when you reach your farthest point you are too tired to do anything but stumble back to the place where you started. This is agony. Besides being unpleasant, it creates a strain on those with whom you are skiing, who may be in better shape. Of course, because your greatest desire is to "get it over with," your technique on the return leg will suffer. Exhaustion leads to lack of coordination, which in turn can lead to injury. This may sound like preaching, but the fact of the matter is that it happens all the time and is totally unnecessary.

Cross-country skiing *is* strenuous. It puts into play virtually every muscle group in your body, as you realize after the first day's trip. Chest and shoulder muscles ache from the pole push. Thigh and calf muscles are sore from the constant stride. Not only do your muscles get a workout, but your entire respiratory system has been functioning much closer to capacity than you ever thought possible. You are breathing much more deeply than you usually do; the body demands oxygen to keep you going. Exhaustion comes when your muscles and lungs can no longer keep up with the work that is demanded of them. Many times, the difference between the winner and those bringing up the rear can be seen in physical clues as they cross the finish line. Except for the short races (10–15 kilometers), which are sprints for top competitors, where everyone is panting from the intensity of it, at the end of a long-distance race the also-rans are crumpling, while the winner and those immediately behind him (or her) usually aren't even breathing hard.

The racer, of course, spends much of his time in training during the winter and may run as much as 20–30 miles a day. He has conquered technique and now is concentrating on endurance. The recreational skier has no reason to train

123

to this extent, or even to push himself to the limit of his endurance. But he should be in acceptable shape so that fatigue doesn't spoil his fun. What is "acceptable" becomes a matter for individual consideration based on the amount of skiing one intends to do. But, theoretically, you ought to be able to spend at least 2–3 relaxing hours on skis and return not completely wrung out, but what might be described as "comfortably tired." While you may not at first be able to complete the entire circuit at the same speed, including pauses to rest, neither should the return trip be one of complete agony.

Just as cross-country skiing is an individual sport based on the depth of one's own involvement, so conditioning also is an individual matter. The only unequivocal statement we make is: You can't rise from a sedentary life that does not include some form of exercise and expect to enjoy cross-country skiing to the same extent as the person who leads a vigorous existence and is in reasonable shape when he or she begins. The body simply cannot cope with the change in effort and the sudden demands that are being made on it. Based on our experience, however, the sedentary person who takes up cross-country is not as common as the one who is involved most of the year in some form of recreational and physical activity. Cross-country skiers tend to be hikers and backpackers during the summer. They ride bicycles and play tennis and golf (if they walk from tee to tee) and swim; in fact, all of these activities are excellent for retaining muscle tone and vigor. Even lawn mowing, despite its enervating aspects, is helpful.

The main consideration in relating one's physical activities to cross-country is that the sport employs the cardio-vascular system to its fullest—and anything during your pre-season physical activities that does the same will aid you in building the stamina you'll want for cross-country. If you *are* a sedentary type, therefore, but expect to take up cross-country skiing and plan to engage in a physical program, it would be wise to hie yourself to your physician for a check-up to see if there is anything you need to guard against. Then, gradually begin your program. Your doctor can help with scheduling.

Here are some ideas for pre-season and on-the-snow conditioning that we have found effective.

PRE-SEASON

If you figure the skiing season as being 5 months long (December–April) at the most, then during the remaining months it's up to you to develop a program that will keep you in condition. Strangely enough, most people seem to have the most difficulty staying in shape during the fall. Summer physical activities have ended, winter activities have not yet begun, and one tends to get lax and lose the muscle tone built up during the previous months. It's easy to avoid this, as we shall see.

Walking and Hiking Most heart specialists will tell you that walking is the easiest form of exercise and the simplest way to retain muscle tone. The problem, of course, is that during most of our daily activities we have a lazy alternative. In other words, it takes a certain amount of willpower to get up half an hour earlier to walk to the train station, or to take a brisk walk after dinner rather than sit around and watch TV. During the work week, find ways of walking rather than riding. Walk to the next appointment in town; walk to your office from your suburban connection; walk home from the train station or bus stop. On weekends, walk a couple of miles each day. When you walk, do it briskly, arms swinging at a good pace. Every day, walk. If you can walk, you can ski. If you walk a lot, you can ski a lot better.

A writer we know whose specialty is big-game hunting often finds himself in New York City for weeks at a time at his editorial desk. He knows that when he's hunting he must keep up with his guides, who make their living in the outdoors. He knows that when the time comes to press the trigger, he can't be so exhausted that his rifle wavers. So every day he climbs the 8 floors to his office, rather than taking the elevator, to stay in condition. This is a rather extreme example, but the point is that using stairs when you can is just another one of those small things you can do each day to stay in shape.

Hiking is walking by another name, but it is just as sweet. Hiking off the beaten path in the woods, mountains, and countryside is the best way we know of to condition oneself for cross-country skiing. Besides the observance of the change of seasons, while hiking one has to surmount terrain changes as well. Climbs, scrambles over loose rock, leaps over streams are all part of hiking and put a strain on the body's different muscle groups, just as cross-country skiing does.

In hiking, try to maintain a steady pace, especially when climbing—not fast, just a regular tempo. It's better to hike at one speed for 50 minutes and take a 10-minute rest break each hour than to saunter along, which has its own rewards but does little to keep you thin.

If you're looking for a place to hike, why not try one of the cross-country trails in your area. It will give you an idea of the terrain you'll be covering in the winter. Or hike over new terrain you might want to scout for touring. Observe the climbs and sidehills you'll have to contend with, as well as the downward gradients. It can make for a pleasant morning or a day's outing. Is there a clearly marked trail? Will any underbrush have to be cut? Is it all bushwhacking? Is there a particular large outcropping that you will be able to use for shelter? All of these observations make hiking less of a chore and more related to your cross-country needs. Longer hikes involve backpacking, and even this is good, because carrying the weight of the pack helps build strength.

Jogging   Much has been written about jogging as a form of conditioning, and there is no question about its validity. The problem with jogging, as it is usually done, is that it is boring. There is a way to counteract this. If you are jogging in town, take a different route each time of approximately the same length. Another problem with jogging is that one not only has to find the time and develop the will to do it, but resist the psychological pressures of one's fellow man, who sees the jogger in the darkness of early morning or at twilight as some kind of nut. You can counter this with a ploy of your own that has always been recommended for preseason conditioning for alpine skiers. Jog through the countryside, across lots, or in the woods. Find routes with interesting terrain. Then trot along, not only on a footpath, but dodging trees, jumping from rock to rock, running up and down hills.

Jogging downhill is better for the thigh and calf muscles and hamstrings and knees than most calisthenic-type exercises because the legs must work against gravity to hold you back. Jog on your toes, pushing back with each step and reaching out with the other leg, arms up or swinging. Again, especially in the fall, jog on the trails or cross-country routes you plan to use when snow comes.

Tennis Of the individual conditioning sports, we consider tennis one of the best. The game not only quickens the reflexes, but, when it is played well, it involves all of the body, especially the legs, which must bend and stretch and keep moving almost all the time. Tennis is no longer a summertime sport. The spread of indoor tennis courts throughout the country is particularly beneficial to the cross-country skier. The weekly 2-hour tennis game is an excellent way to prepare for weekend touring.

Bicycling Bicycling has become an integral part of the U.S. National Cross-Country Team's pre-season training program, and it's easy to understand why. Bicycling has much in common with cross-country. Both depend upon rhythm and balance. In bicycling, as in other conditioning activities we've mentioned, most of the body's muscle groups are engaged. For the cross-country participant, bicycling is not hard to take. It's another form of touring, which helps to explain its sudden rise in popularity. Daily use of a bicycle for errands and for local transportation will pay off when winter comes and you're ready to take that first cross-country jaunt. Better a bicycle than a second car—it's cheaper and it's good for you, besides. Extend your trips if you can, and don't hesitate to bicycle uphill. The climbs build wind and strengthen your calf and thigh muscles.

Some Thoughts on Calisthenics and Team Sports A lot has been made, in books and in the ski press, of pre-season calisthenics as a way of getting ready for on-snow activity. Our own opinion is that for the recreational skier, conditioning exercises, while useful if they are already part of the daily routine, are not necessary if a good program of daily physical activity is carried out. There are those who swear by aerobics and RCAF exercises, and there is no doubt that their value is proven. But conditioning exercises imply a routine that is sometimes quite difficult to follow. The physical activity we have suggested, which can be integrated into one's normal pattern, is often easier to handle and, for the recreational tourer, will have the same end result—the development of stamina.

For those who are seriously considering racing, however, a set daily period of limbering and strengthening calisthenics can be useful. Pay particular attention to leg and thigh exercises that develop flexibility and strength. Sit-ups and push-ups are always useful, especially the latter for arms and shoulders that take a large amount of strain. The advice of a competent coach or physical therapist can be useful in prescribing the appropriate exercises. For cross-country, one does not need the heavy bunched muscles of the football player, but the long lean ones typical of the runner and swimmer.

For youngsters engaged in team sports, there is no substitute for soccer as a conditioner for skiing. It is not by accident that many of the national Alpine and Nordic team members are active soccer players. Soccer is a game of constant movement, quick reactions, cuts, turns, and stops. It builds endurance and is highly recommended.

ONCE THE SEASON STARTS

Like most other sports, the adage about not overdoing it holds for cross-country skiing as well. Beginners will find that their initial treks are self-limiting anyway; 2 hours for the first few on-snow tours will probably be as much as they can take without strain. With experience comes the ability to run for longer distances on more varied terrain.

129

But those who are beyond the novice stage should also gradually work up to their distance running. One way to do this, before engaging in lengthy day trips, is to ski a set circuit of a given number of miles on succeeding outings and try to beat the time of the previous outing. There are several advantages to this. It gives the skier the opportunity to experiment with waxes for different types of snow and weather, because conditions are never the same on succeeding days and, in fact, are not always the same during the circuit. It helps develop technique so that a steady pace can be kept using whatever strides and maneuvers are needed to cope with the changes in terrain. And, of course, it helps build stamina.

In considering what sort of course to lay out and run, it is suggested that it be divided into thirds—roughly one-third straight running, one-third climbing, and one-third downhill. Obviously the track need not be straight—there should be turns and dips, downhill stretches with turning runouts, passages through woods, across footbridges, around and over knolls, and so forth. This kind of course provides variety and makes the self-imposed training quite interesting.

Skiing your local golf course may sound tame, but the typical 18-hole layout, from tee to tee, extends about 7000 yards, which is a considerable distance for a morning's workout. Bunkers and traps hidden by the snow can become good gradients, long fairways make for extended straight courses, and usually there are woods through which you can pass if you want to try your technique in deeper snow.

Bridle paths in suburban reservations and parks that are not usually used in the wintertime make good cross-country trails. They are cleared of underbrush, are quite wide, and generally have enough changes in the terrain, although gradual, to provide interesting touring circuits. Both golf courses and bridle paths allow the skier to come back to his starting point, even though the circuit may be roundabout.

Some transmission line cuts can be used for touring, although you will probably have to double back on yourself to return to the starting point. Country roads are also good if the snow is deep enough to be packed down without going through to the gravel or blacktop. If not, take to the countryside—loose gravel, even if brought to the surface, will raise havoc with ski bottoms.

Five to seven miles is a reasonable distance for running during your initial training periods. Once you can accomplish this stretch comfortably, you can go on to longer routes and day trips without fear of falling behind.

The question of comfort also has to do with proper clothing. Even on short trips, it's useful to dress in layers with your outer garment a light one—such as a poplin or nylon anorak. We've mentioned that your body, with its enginelike efficiency, will become superheated. After a mile or two, unless it's severely cold, you'll be skiing with your anorak tied around your waist. One tip: If you're resting outdoors for any length of time, put the anorak back on. Unprotected by that impervious layer of cotton or nylon, your body will lose its heat very quickly and you will become chilled and stiff. This applies to lunch breaks in cold weather especially. And after skiing, a hot shower or sauna as soon as possible will keep you from becoming chilled and help keep the muscles loose.

Don't forget to limber up before starting on your trek. Loosen up the arms and legs by shaking them. Do a few knee bends before putting on skis. Don't stride right off; do a few skating turns and other maneuvers to loosen up, especially when the weather is cold.

If the temperature is in the teens or below and the wind is up, constantly check for frostbite on cheeks, nose, and ears. The wind-chill factor brings the temperature that affects you well below the thermometer reading. Watch for white patches on those that accompany you and have them keep an eye on you as well. In cold weather, with the possibility of a snowstorm brewing, always ski with at least one or two other persons if you are planning to be out for any length of time away from shelter. If there are signs of frostbite, don't rub, but cover the affected area with a bare or gloved hand. If fingertips start feeling numb, rotate your arms violently in a circle to force the blood into your fingertips to keep the blood circulating through the tiny capillaries there.

PREPARING YOUR EQUIPMENT FOR CROSS-COUNTRY SKIING

AFTER SKIING

Most skiers make it a rule to clean the snow off the skis and bindings, wipe off the remaining moisture, and then scrape the surface wax off the ski bottoms down to the base-impregnating coat. This gives you the opportunity of seeing whether the base coat needs to be touched up. It also gets the skis ready for the new surface wax you'll be applying before the next outing.

Boots should be wiped dry and, if wet inside, stuffed with newspaper to absorb the moisture. Ordinary shoe polish is the best protective coating for boots. A soft wax sold commercially can be applied to the stitching where uppers and soles are joined to prevent snow and moisture from infiltrating. Skis need not be blocked if they're being used frequently (once a week or so) but should be stored in a dry place between uses. Leaning them against a wall with tips up is satisfactory. Poles require very little care other than checking baskets for damage; a broken or missing basket on the trail prevents proper use of the pole. Clothing, of course, should be dried out thoroughly, but don't place nylon garments on a hot radiator.

AFTER THE SEASON

Between seasons, cross-country skis, because they are made of wood, need the most care. Some tips:

1. Store skis in a dry place where the air circulates freely.
2. Wood skis should be blocked. The object is to make sure that they retain their camber until they are used again. Without blocking they will tend to flatten out unequally and lose the spring that camber provides. To block them, simply place a block of wood roughly the width of the skis between the ski soles at the highest point of camber—usually underneath the bindings. Fasten the skis sole to sole with rubber ski ties or cord. To increase camber, move the ties closer to the block; to decrease camber, move the ties closer to the tips and heels of the skis. Thickness of the wood block is determined by the body weight of the skier. A 2-inch thickness should be the maximum required to hold the camber of a heavy person's skis.
3. Before blocking, check the camber. When you're in the bindings on a level floor, you should be able to slide a sheet of newspaper between the ski soles and the floor. If you can't, there is too little cam-

ber, and it should be increased. Fastening the skis sole to sole allows equal adjustment in the camber of both skis.

4. If you are really confident about your ability with a blowtorch, one way of ensuring camber adjustment is to heat the skis lightly with the torch before blocking.

Bindings should be coated with light oil before storage. Boots need the same sort of care you give your own shoes—polish with regular shoe polish and make sure they are stored in a dry place to avoid mildew. Poles should be hung out of the way, also in a dry storage area.

There is no reason why your cross-country equipment shouldn't be cared for properly, and it will save a lot of grief when the new season begins. Remember that cross-country skis are much more delicate and subject to moisture and temperature changes in storage than their modern alpine metal or fiberglass counterparts. When the season starts, you'll be glad you took proper care of your equipment.

6 A Day's Tour

PUTTING IT ALL TOGETHER

Downhill skiers know that the snow season doesn't end on Washington's Birthday. In fact, if snow depths are good, the nights are cold, and occasional snowstorms drop new powder, the best skiing of all is in March and April. Then come rare days of long-lasting sun and deep blue skies when it's possible to be out from dawn until the last slanting golden hours of late afternoon.

Spring is the best time for touring, too. While snow conditions can be very variable, putting a premium on your knowledge of soft waxes, subzero temperatures and high winds are no longer a problem. The weather tends to stabilize into continuous days of sunshine and cloudless skies, providing shirtsleeve touring conditions. These are touring days that linger in the memory, and you should be ready to make the most of them.

For a good part of the winter, you've spent the weekends practicing near your home or at a cross-country center. You've taken longer and longer routes with mixed terrain at a fairly steady pace. Downhill stretches on the trail no longer have you baffled; you find you can stop or turn at will as you run out. You can climb without becoming utterly exhausted. You've taken some off-trail runs in new snow and find breaking trail, although tiring, less difficult than you had thought it would be.

In fact, you've become so accomplished at cross-country that you find it hard to remember your own clumsiness at the start of the season. So, with a March weekend in the offing, you decide on a day's tour—a kind of graduation trip with friends—lunch on the trail, a day of sun and snow.

In planning your tour, here are some considerations to keep in mind before you go out and when you're on snow:

EQUIPMENT AND ACCESSORIES YOU SHOULD HAVE: A CHECKLIST

Rucksacks   Each skier should have one, so that gear can be shared equally among the touring party.

Wax Kit   Include a scraper. One kit per person. During the typical spring tour, conditions will change depending upon average temperature and the amount of sunshine. Snow conditions can go from crust at dawn to breakable crust, to corn snow, to hard-pack again as the day progresses. Or if the temperature early in the morning is at the freezing mark and the day is to be sunny, there is a good chance that by noon, terrain that is sheltered and hit by the sun directly will become slushy. On the other hand, shady trails protected from the sun by trees will not require the same waxing as open cross-country courses. Similarly, if it is a partly cloudy day and the temperature is hovering around the freezing point, when the sun disappears the snow will tend to harden. The cross-country skier should be prepared for all of these eventualities and be ready to wax en route. Our rule applies, both when starting out and during the day: Wax for the coldest snow you think you'll find, then apply softer waxes as needed over the harder base. After lunch is a good time to rewax, figuring that the warmest time of the day is between 12 noon and 2 P.M. and that it will grow progressively colder as the afternoon wears on.

First Aid Kit   At least one kit should be carried by the group. The small boating or auto packs are light and useful. To the basic gauze, bandaids, aspirin, and the like, add the following:

> a lightweight blanket
> metal mirror, for signaling
> tongue depressors, for finger splints
> tweezers
> suntan cream, lip balm, etc.

Small Tools   Here are some which have proved useful.

> pliers
> screwdriver
> electrician's tape

To the above, used mainly for repairing bindings and skis, add such safety equipment as:

137

flashlights (or cross-country headlamps)

extra metal ski tips

mini transistor radio (good for tuning into local weather reports)

small ax for chopping kindling

newspaper; a few pages will help in starting a fire when crumpled up. (Purists will argue this point, but take the newspaper anyway.)

matches—several small boxes

small compass. The typical huntsman's compass is eminently useful, especially if the weather changes and it begins to snow hard and you lose the trail. These compasses are inexpensive (about $6.50) and should be part of every tourer's kit.

marking flags—if snow threatens but you're starting anyway, they're useful for placing along the trail to mark your return route. They can be purchased at ski equipment shops. They're small, and your group should take about 100 of them.

Clothing   You should always be prepared for weather changes and the possibility of a drop in temperature. Carry:

extra gloves

extra net undershirt

poplin or nylon shell (light anorak). You should wear it during rest stops to avoid becoming chilled.

one pair of dry socks

gaiters, if you are planning to ski in deeper snow

Food   Your problem is twofold: what sort of food to take and how to cook it.

For your first trip, pre-pack a picnic lunch of sandwiches or fried chicken. Freeze-dried foods, although expensive, are available in camping supply stores and are delicious, although they take more time to prepare than pre-packed meals. Freeze-dried soups, packaged instant coffee, and nondairy cream can be brought along. If you're planning to cook, a small saucepan should be carried, also some plastic utensils—they're light and disposable. Take *several* pocket knives. They seem to disappear when you need them.

Someone is going to have to carry the wine; what spring tour would be complete without it?

Don't forget the fire-building materials. Some tour leaders carry pieces of light kindling in the rucksacks, but pine branches are just as useful for the same purpose. When building a fire, dig a hole in the snow about 1- or 2-feet deep. The rim of snow around the fire supports heavy branches for holding a cook pot in place and also protects the flame from the wind. Melt snow for boiling water. The Scandinavians have taught us much of what we know about day touring, including the usefulness of fir boughs. Spread on the snow, they make a kind of aromatic blanket between you and the cold surface—especially when placed on the bottoms of your skis. Three cross-country skis placed bindings-down on the snow make an excellent "bench" to sit on when you're having lunch. Make sure that the binding mechanism is free of snow when you start out again. And, of course, before you cut pine branches, make sure it's legal and has been cleared with the property owner, state forest ranger, or other local authorities. When lunch is finished, use a plastic bag for garbage; you will have to carry it back to the nearest disposal point. Burying it, obviously, is meaningless; it will only be there to clutter up the wilderness when the snow melts.

The fire will have burned deeper into its hole and shoveling snow over it will put it out. But inspect it carefully to make sure you've left no burning embers.

THE TOUR: SOME THOUGHTS TO KEEP IN MIND

Cross-country touring is the winter version of backpacking and hiking, and although the principles of leadership are the same, there are a number of important differences. Most are based on common sense but are worth emphasizing for the first-time tourer.

In common with hiking tours, there should be one leader who has some knowledge of the outdoors, is the best of the skiers, and is able to remain cool if an emergency situation arises. It is important that other members of the party recognize that, on the trail, his word is law. In covering more difficult terrain, he should be in the van. For instance, if the trail takes a curving drop where the runout cannot be seen from above, he should make the run first, then guide the other skiers down to his point. His knowledge of cross-country technique should be such that he can suggest to less-skilled members of the group how to tackle terrain that seems difficult for them. In touring untracked snow, he need not break trail continually; this chore should be divided among the members of the party. And he should designate another good skier to bring up the rear of the group so that no one is ever left floundering behind.

A viable tour party should consist of at least 3 persons and probably not more than 8 to avoid stringing skiers all over the landscape. Three, as the smallest number, recognizes the possibility of injury and allows one person to stay with the injured party while the fastest skier goes back for help. The touring group should never move faster than its slowest member and this fact should be carefully considered when the tour is being organized. There is absolutely no point in having a party of good skiers taking along a novice unless everyone is willing to be slowed down considerably. In our experience, despite the good intentions of the better skiers, an unbalanced group creates tension; the fast skiers want to move at a good pace and the slow skier is constantly apologizing for his lack of technique or ability, finally resorting to a kind of benumbed silence when tiredness overtakes him. When this happens, he will fall frequently and be unable to keep up, with resultant strain on the remainder of the group.

It's up to the leader to set the pace and make a judgment on how frequently the group should rest. This judgment must also include the length of the tour and the kind of terrain the tour will cover. The tendency is to take on more than the group can accomplish—especially on one of those spring days when it seems that nothing can fail and everything is possible. If it is a first outing, less is better. Everyone will then want to come back for more.

In skiing with the family, Dad is the leader and exerts the authority of his office in keeping the eagerness of the children in bounds. Children tend to have spurts of energy; they want to explore, to wander off the trail, to move on ahead. Within reason, this should be curbed, and they should be adjured to stay with the group. Despite their energy, children, especially younger ones, tire easily, and the length of the trip and its route should be considered carefully. A short trip can be made to appear like a long outing if a lunch break is planned at the midway point with adequate time for the youngsters to rest. Two hours out and two hours back is a safe maximum, especially for starters. Remember, too, children get chilled more easily than adults; they should wear more layers, even though they will probably peel them, but they should cover up during rest breaks and lunchtime. Allow them to carry their own rucksacks and to break trail, if only for short periods. Stop to point out natural signs along the way; animal tracks can be identified by youngsters who have studied up on them prior to the tour.

In choosing untracked terrain, if that's your plan, a contour map of the area is a necessity in deciding your route. Contour maps are marked off in intervals of 10 feet; the closer the intervals are to each other, the steeper the terrain. Pick gradual terrain for climbing so that you can traverse and turn, if necessary, rather than having to herringbone up steep slopes. A long gradual climb to a ridge line is more fun than having to fight ledges. The map should be as complete as possible, with landmarks, farms, and houses clearly indicated. All cross-country centers supply such maps of their areas for both marked trails and possible off-trail touring.

The tour leader should be weather-wise. Pay attention to local forecasts before you leave. They will have a decided effect on the route you take and the kind of terrain you choose. If snow is forecast, stay on marked trails. If the day is sunny but the forecast calls for "local flurries" later in the day, keep an eye on the sky and watch for changes. Clouds moving in and a change in wind direction may mean snow. Flurries can be very heavy at times, with sudden decreases in visibility. In case of doubt, play it safe and head back along the route you have taken, following your own tracks, or the ribbons you have attached to trees, or the flags you've planted in the snow if you've been smart.

Unless you know the terrain, sudden snow squalls are not pleasant. They're usually accompanied by a drop in temperature, and even if you're a short distance from your destination, getting back becomes a fight. Squalls are a fact of life in higher altitudes; the leader must keep himself oriented at all times. It's totally important, in falling snow, to keep the party together. A distance of 3 ski lengths between skiers is a safe one.

Along with cross-country touring come some rather peculiar problems. How do you climb over a fence, for instance? A wire fence takes 2 people. Depending upon the distance of the top strand from the snow, either the leader presses his skis down on the wire so that the next skier can step over it, or he holds the top and second strand apart so that the skier can slip between them. This continues until the last skier has passed through. It's not considered good form to cut a farmer's wire fence, although snowmobilers do it more times than not. If the top bar of a wood fence is low enough, you can literally ski over it, with the help of your poles. Otherwise, use your poles to help you side step over it, keeping your skis parallel to the fence.

Here are some other tips to help you counter almost any sort of terrain and snow conditions you will run into:

Bumps and Ruts   If it's a downhill section, learn to ride your skis with one of them slightly ahead of the other. It will help your balance and also give you a springboard for a change in direction via a skating or stem turn. If there's a rutted track, stay in the ruts; you'll move along faster. But be prepared to skate or step out of them if you're gliding on a downhill section of the track.

Soft Snow   This applies to areas where snows are deep. Stay away from what appear to be young evergreens. They may be the *tops* of trees. And the area around them is going to be quite soft and sinkable. This is a common problem in the West.

143

Snow Hummocks   Careful. They may be felled logs, tree stumps, and the like, and will splinter your skis if you run into them with any force.

Snow Bridges   In the United States, these are usually formed over creeks and streams, although in the high Alps they hide crevasses. In crossing a stream, use your pole to test the thickness of the snow; it may be a thin layer with water rushing underneath, or it may solidly cover a frozen portion of the stream.

Wooded Areas   We recommend in skiing through the woods, especially if there is underbrush or low-hanging branches, that the hands be removed from the pole straps. It's easy to catch the pole basket on a branch, and the sudden jerk on the arm, if you catch the pole basket, can dislocate a shoulder. This becomes very important on downhill passages through the trees when you are carrying a great deal of momentum.

Wood Bridges   In the spring the snow on them melts before it does on the ground. An acquaintance of ours who should have known better was gliding rather quickly down an inclined portion of the trail that led to a wooden bridge over a stream. So bemused was he by the scenery and the gloriousness of it all that he forgot to look ahead and was stopped rather suddenly as he slid over the last remaining section of snow on the trail and hit the bridge. So sudden was the stop that his momentum carried him over the side into the stream, from where he was finally rescued by the last member of the tour party, who heard some interesting, if indelicate, words issuing from under the bridge as he picked his way along the boards.

The moral of this anecdote is: *Always look ahead,* and be prepared to stop, turn, or do whatever is needed to handle the terrain satisfactorily. Keep your eyes on the trail and your head up, and stay in control.

THE TOURING EXPERIENCE

This account of a day's tour is based not on a single day's happenings, but on a number of like cross-country trips made by one of the authors. It is a composite of experiences on the trail. And while the locale is Vermont, it might just as well be the Midwest, or Upper New York State, or northern California—or anywhere there is enough snow to make tracks.

There are some skiing days during which nothing but good can take place. On this certain day in mid-March, it has been decided to take a long tour in the vicinity of a ski area in northern Vermont. Our circuit will be in the hills that slope down from a mountain that is one of the anchors of the Green Mountain chain. When, early in the morning, sunlight filters through the windows, we know that the continuous snowstorms of the past several days have ended and that we are in for a rare treat.

It has been a record spring—days on end of gray skies and constantly falling snow. We have agreed to meet on the first clear morning for a cross-country tour that will not involve much bushwhacking but will take us on a roundabout series of trails that has already been marked by an expert friend who has agreed to act as tour leader. There will be a certain amount of trail breaking involved. But now, with the day starting out cold and the snow fresh, it is unlikely that we will have much difficulty with the terrain.

Each of us has been asked to bring his own rucksack and gear. Anticipating a change in the weather, I have lain everything out the evening before, ready to pack if the sun should finally appear: extra socks, wax kit and scraper, extra sweater, wool hat, a first-aid kit.

No waxing has been done yet. I have no idea of the consistency of the snow or the range of the day's temperature at this early hour, even though the sunlight seems to indicate a bluebird day. It is not warm, however; the thermometer outside our kitchen window registers 15 degrees. But if the range is not more than another 15 degrees and stays below the freezing mark, we are going to have perfect skiing without having to bother with klister waxes. In any case, Sverre's workshop is fully equipped with extra waxes, a burner, and whatever tools we might need.

Cold meats and cheese will be the food for the day plus instant coffee and cocoa for warmth and wine for good cheer. Oranges are ready to be packed; I have found from experience that they are both energy-giving and refreshing on the trail. Also waiting is a chocolate-raisin candy bar and a Swedish sailor's knife, razor sharp and sheathed. And the all-important corkscrew.

Skis have been scraped down to the impregnating base, bindings checked for loose screws. When in the morning Sverre's cheerful phone call comes, there is little to do but place the gear in the rucksack. Coffee and toast and some scrambled eggs suffice for breakfast. The rucksack is tossed in the back of the station wagon with the skis and poles, and we are off—a 20-minute drive to the leader's house.

Sverre is waiting with cups of steaming coffee. Fresh ski tracks outside his door tell the story. "Absolutely great this morning," he says. "I have been out for an hour already while you were still asleep, breaking trail so you won't have to work so hard." He laughs. "It's too nice a day to work hard."

I find that we are to be a party of 7, all of whom have had considerable alpine skiing experience, although some are relatively new to cross-country. There is a young couple from Baltimore, a friend who works at the ski area, and 2 charming young waitresses from one of the ski lodges.

We sip coffee and discuss the wax. "Like the sky," Sverre says. "blue. But take some red along in case it gets warmer. We can always wax again at lunchtime." He offers to melt in wax for anyone who wants it. An artist with the burner, he flicks the flame above the ski bottoms so that the wax flows evenly. Then, with a cork, he burnishes it in. There is the pungent smell of wax in the room.

I decide to wax my skis outside. It is 9:15, and with the sun still at a low angle, the birches and the firs throw soft blue shadows on the snow. In the open, where there are no trees, the myriad crystals of new powder are caught by the sun like so many diamond facets.

It is a silent world at this hour, broken only by a raucous commotion in one of the trees, where two blue jays are chasing each other. One of them breaks off his argument and, unafraid, lands within 10 feet of me, hoping for a hand-out, no doubt. These are the ubiquitous "camp robbers," friends of the outdoorsman and the skier. In the spring they hang about the outdoor sundeck of the ski area's cafeteria and will eat almost anything, including the apple pie off your plate.

I unroll the wrap off the stick of blue and apply the wax in short strokes, remembering not to get it in the groove. Then I use the burnishing cork until the wax looks slick on the ski bottom. For a finishing touch, I use the heel of my hand. I know that the wax may not last as long as for those who have melted it in, but because the snow is new and not very cold, it won't be as abrasive as the old crusty variety or even new snow that has fallen in below-zero temperatures. I lean the skis against the side of the house to let the wax harden and go inside for another cup of coffee.

A discussion is taking place concerning the route. Sverre says he knows a spot sheltered by a grove of trees where we can stop for lunch. We examine his contour map. It is mostly uphill getting there, about a 2½-hour jaunt. But there are some straight sections to vary the climb. Coming back, we will take a different route with other problems, gradually making our way home downhill, because we are apt to be more tired in the afternoon. We will be on the trail for approximately 5 hours, which will get us back with the late rays of the sun. Sverre, with the wisdom of the experienced, packs a flashlight anyway. His rucksack is the heaviest; he has decided to bring some dry kindling along for the lunchtime fire. Two of us divide the food and another takes the jug of Mountain Red.

Outside now, there is a bustle of activity. Others have placed their skis near mine to let the wax harden. Now they take them down and slip into them and adjust the bindings. Rucksacks are slung over shoulders. The two girls skate off and make a big circle and come back. I get into my skis, grasp the poles, and slide away. It takes me about 100 yards to start feeling the rhythm again. Then I make a step turn where the trail narrows near a group of trees and return to the group. Now others are doing it as we wait for the last of the group to clamp down their bindings. We shuffle around until legs feel loose and the body starts pumping adrenaline.

The girl from Baltimore is giggling. She has tried to edge on a small sidehill as if she were on alpine skis, but the

skis slide out from under her. She realizes there are no steel
edges to set; the feel of the skis is different. She falls and
gets up and falls again, and it all seems very funny. Her
husband says, "You'll get used to it. Just stay in my tracks."
They ski off together. He seems to have developed a nice
stride. Intent on following his rhythm, she slowly stretches
into a stride of her own. When they return, she says, "I
think I've got it." Her laugh infects us all. It is going to be
a merry day.

We adjust each other's rucksacks so that they ride as high
as possible. Sverre, in his bright red Norwegian print
sweater, leads off, and the group uncoils behind him. Tailing
the group, I have the advantage of skiing in the tracks everyone else has made, along with the responsibility of herding
the stragglers along. It is 10 A.M.

At the outset, Sverre sets a slow pace to give everyone the
feel of the snow and of their skis. The trail follows a slight
grade. We can use the diagonal stride, although the pressure
in our legs tells us that we are climbing gradually around the
bend of a hill. It is all open slope, and the sun, to our left
and somewhat behind us, lies warm on our backs. In effect,
we are climbing to a tree-covered ridge. We will pass
through the trees once we get there on a long straight run
atop the ridge, then begin a steeper climb to the crest of
another hill, where the trail again follows the ridge line to
a kind of open plateau. Then the trail dips into a forest.
Somewhere along the forest passage is Sverre's lunch stop.

This is typical Vermont countryside. We are crossing
what were farm lots. But in this part of the state the farmers
have left the land or sold it off to developers, and the forest
is gradually encroaching on fields that had been tilled since
the first settlers came to Vermont before the Revolutionary
War.

Following the group, which is now strung out so that there are 3 or 4 ski lengths between each person, I muse on the changes that have been wrought on Vermont. These empty farm lots seem an example of how Vermonters have traded away their birthright, land, to the point where non-residents hold title to most of it. Not far from here, in one town, residents own only 3000 acres of the town's 28,000. Skiers or developers or giant lumber companies own the rest.

We will not pass any of the tiny deserted graveyards that dot some of Vermont's uplands that residents have long since left. But I am reminded of two of them that tell much about what Vermont was. In one small town nearby, markers in the graveyard tell of Vermont's boys killed in the Civil War, members of the First Vermont Brigade who died at Gettysburg.

And in another, near Chittenden, there are several rows of tiny stones that tell the tale of a diphtheria epidemic that decimated parts of the state in 1840. Reflecting on this history, it seems to me that we have literally imposed another civilization on what was here. An urban horde has descended upon original America in the name of recreation. And we have bent what was here into our own image, finally, with the consent of the native. I think of Robert Penn Warren's lines about Vermont:

> . . . *Can't help but remember that if there are only*
> *Sixteen voters and one dies, that leaves only*
> *Fifteen.* . . .

Not that we skiers have been all bad for Vermont. We have turned marginal farming communities into boom towns and perhaps have helped prevent the drain of manpower that was slowly filtering out of the state. But we have also helped desecrate the land, too, until stopped by some fierce ecology laws. Now somehow it seems that in cross-country touring we are quietly paying a tribute to the land that was—using the terrain without tearing it up for private gain.

We file through the trees—an ancient maple or "sugar bush" stand by the looks of it, with old V-shaped scars marking the trees where some farmer tapped for the makings of syrup. Below us there were probably the ruins of a sugar house where giant vats, constantly tended by a farmhand, used to boil off the sap. A whole life once echoed in these quiet woods—the bells of oxen hauling sugar sleds, the shouts of men urging them along. Up here now, all is stillness as our skis move along the trail. Everyone, it seems, is caught up by the atmosphere.

Ahead the trail widens below a steep hill, and the group, from single file, merges into a clump gathered around Sverre. We have, surprisingly, been skiing for an hour, and Sverre decides to call a rest break. The slope directly faces the sun, and we shed our rucksacks and sit on them. With the pack removed, my whole body seems infinitely lighter and I feel that I will be able to waft my way up the slope with unusual speed.

Sverre says, "This is as far as I got this morning, so we'll have to break trail until we link up with the Red Trail, which someone else has been skiing this morning. Anyway, we'll earn our lunch." No one seems to mind. Everyone has been keeping up well.

When we start again, I move behind Sverre to help break trail. We have shed our anoraks and put them in our rucksacks. The girl from Baltimore has tied hers around her waist, and part of it droops across her derriere. "In case I fall." She laughs and her joy makes us all smile.

One of the others takes a handful of snow and sucks on it. The snow is still soft and consistent. Even though we are warm, the temperature is still in the twenties, and the snow hasn't begun to consolidate yet. By tomorrow, if this weather remains the same, the powder will become much heavier and cementlike. Breaking trail will really become a chore.

This morning, however, it is difficult enough. We are no longer striding, but making a series of zigzags up the slope. The technique is a kind of trudge in which the poles become all-important—one ski forward, then the other ski. It helps to hold the hands higher on the poles, pushing with a flick of the wrist on each pole-aided step.

At the end of one traverse, Sverre does a kick turn and starts his climb to the next level. I make mine, not without stumbling as I bring one ski around, and follow him. Halfway across, he stops and regards the rest of the group, knowing what is going to happen. Kick turns are not part of the alpine skier's repertoire anymore, and although some of the party are able to accomplish a reasonable facsimile of a kick turn, there is quite a bit of sitting down and more laughter. One of the men shuns the kick turn and steps around. It is all ok. In cross-country, anything goes.

We have 2 more traverses to make to bring us out atop the plateau that will be the highest point of our tour. I am perspiring profusely. Gloves have been removed and are tucked under the waistband of my knickers. Just having the cool air on my hands is refreshing. We pause for a moment and I wipe some snow across my face and then continue to follow Sverre's measured pace.

Our gain in altitude can't be more than several hundred feet, and yet I am starting to feel tired. Sverre moves along as if he could climb to the very top of the mountain that looms ahead of us. He is like a machine. "That's what it means," I think, "to be on skis all of your life." My envy of his ability and lack of fatigue are tinged with a measure of anger at his perfection. I know I am panting more than I should be.

We reach the top almost together, and I see that he too is perspiring; there are droplets of moisture on his forehead. "Good climb." He smiles. "From now on it's all downhill."

We take another break as the group slowly catches up. The sun, at noon, is as high as it will be for the day. Over the mountain, a few wisps of clouds are gathering, indicating some change of weather in the making. But the remainder of the sky is blue. With our exertions we are hot. Underneath my sweater I can feel the dampness of my turtleneck shirt and wonder why I wore it.

Now we can see the entire valley clearly. Far off is the Wren-steepled church of the village with several white-painted houses nestled around it. Across the valley is another range of hills, and a plume of smoke drifts out of the trees. There is a working maple stand there, and the farmer may be getting his sugar-house fire built. A jet contrail makes a pencil-thin line across the sky—a fighter perhaps, from Plattsburg, or the Montreal–New York run. To us below, these signs of another life seem rather unimportant.

On the plateau, a high farm lot, we see several blue flags on stakes. They mark our trail and lead to the fir grove that will be our lunch stop. Sverre sets out and lengthens into the diagonal stride, and we make a long column behind him. I am having trouble now with clumps of snow that cling to the bottoms of my skis, and wish I had taken advantage of his offer to melt in my wax. I scrape the bottom of one ski against the raised upper edge of the other one and then switch. I also find that my socks are wet near the boot tops and remember that I debated whether to wear gaiters but decided against them.

After cleaning my skis, I end up at the tail of the column

153

again. We are spaced over a longer distance than before, with everyone trying to keep pace. But we are struggling a little bit because of fatigue. At the end of the column, keeping in the track, I am able to change up from time to time and double pole. It's restful for the arms. With a sweeping flourish that belies my tiredness, I slide into the picnic spot and free myself of rucksack and skis.

Our grove is a sort of open-ended semicircle, and Sverre already has dug a hole in the center of it. Into the hole go some fresh fir branches and the kindling and then some heavier downed limbs, and the fire is well started. A pot filled with snow is placed on 3 limbs laid across the top of the hole; the melted snow will be used for making coffee.

We take everyone's skis and place them bottom up in sets of 3 around the semicircle and cover them with more fir branches. Now we have benches to sit upon out of the snow. Out of a rucksack comes the Mountain Red, and the wine bottle is passed around. More fir branches are laid down and the food spread out upon it; there is bread and salami and other cold meats and a large hunk of Emmenthaler cheese.

We sit in the sun and eat, in a daze of perfect contentment, feeling, each of us, that we *have* accomplished something quite satisfactory this morning. As far as we are concerned, there is no other world than the semicircular one we are in. Someone relates the Greek legend about the last of the wine; the person who drinks it will soon get married or fall in love. There is a large cheer when one of the waitresses tips up the bottle and lets the last drops trickle onto her tongue.

There is instant tea, instant coffee, and cocoa for those who want it. We sip our coffee, loath to leave this perfect spot. But it is now 2:00, and someone notices that the clouds that have been gathering over the mountain are now more widespread, and, although the sun is still very much with us, we know that it is quite possible for it to start snowing again. We want to enjoy skiing in the sun while we can.

Putting out the fire is simply a matter of filling in the hole with snow and tramping it down. The consistency of the snow hasn't changed too much, and, in fact, it will be getting colder toward the shank of the afternoon, so I rub in some blue over the remains of this morning's wax. There will be little climbing on the way home, which aids my decision.

The return route begins with another straight run through the trees, then a passage over a brook, then a slow but steady drop where the trail joins another route. After that the terrain is varied with one interesting schuss to a footbridge. Then a short climb and another straight back home.

Starting again is almost like beginning in the morning, except that everyone's rucksack is slightly lighter. Two of the men hold an impromptu race, ski off, do quick skating turns around, and ski back. We shuffle tentatively to warm up, and then Sverre moves out in front. Everyone is a bit silly from the wine, and there is some useless sliding until we establish the rhythm. There is an imperceptible drop to the trail—enough to allow double poling with a good glide. I am rear guard again, which allows me to set my own pace. The skier in front of me is one of the waitresses. I notice, as I did this morning, that she rarely falters—just keeps up a steady stride that moves her along without much apparent effort.

Up front the group begins to close ranks and stop. When I catch up, everyone is watching Sverre cross the brook. With the thaw of spring, water has worked its way through the snow cover. But slightly to the left of the trail he has found a snow bridge that extends from one side of the stream to the other. He slides across it slowly, testing the snow with his poles. Then he side steps up the other bank. We do the same, gingerly side stepping down the near bank, taking a big side step across a rivulet to the snow bridge, then slowly skiing to the other side. No one wants to get wet, even though it wouldn't be serious. But ice might form on the ski bottoms, which would have to be scraped off, and wet feet might mean a change of socks—holding up the progress of the group.

The pace quickens across the field until we come to another passage through the trees. This time there is a definite drop to the trail. Sverre pushes off. Standing firm on his skis, knees bent, poles ready, he glides out of sight. We wait at the top until we hear him yell, "Come on. There's a run-out here." The next person takes off. There is a shriek as she begins to pick up speed; then, afraid of falling, she decides to sit down on her skis. It isn't good form, but it's fun. Everyone else opts for good form, but not everyone makes it standing up.

We come out of the woods where our route joins the Blue Trail. Other skiers have been using it today, so it is nicely packed.

It seems strange to see other skiers in the distance. We have been so isolated on our hilltop, even if only for a few hours, that seeing them jolts us back to reality. We don't really want them to break the spell that has carried us into the woods from the start. But they disappear down the trail and we are again alone.

Now there is a passage through a birch grove. It is all sidehill, and there are a number of tracks through the trees where skiers have taken different routes down. Some are steeper than others where the better skiers have been. We also make our own tracks. Sverre demonstrates the "birch-tree stop"; he grabs the trunk of a tree as he slides by it and swings completely around. Someone forgets to duck, and a tasseled Scandinavian hat swings gently on a branch.

I find myself trying to control my speed, but as there really isn't enough room to snowplow and I can't check with a little heel push as I would on alpine skis, I just decide to let them run, slowing myself by dragging my poles. I have removed the pole straps from my wrists to keep from snagging a branch or stump. Then a birch suddenly appears in my path. Rather than sit down, I grab for it, cushioning the shock as I embrace the tree trunk, my skis spread-eagled on both sides of it. I am totally pinned, but I am laughing so hard that it doesn't matter. I can't swing my skis around and I can't back up, so I lift one ski and take it off and, still grasping the tree trunk, bring my uphill leg around. Then standing with my downhill ski across the gradient, I slip into the other one.

The others are waiting as I emerge from the trees. They have been watching from below and commenting on my lack of form. Someone says, "Why didn't you take the tree with you?"

"Very funny," I reply, brushing particles of birchbark off my sweater.

The sun begins to dip behind the mountain, and there are long shadows everywhere. There is a peculiarity about the light this afternoon; it is golden, the trees are lit with it, and we feel the magic of the late afternoon.

Our next challenge is a rather steep hill that we can take in one long schuss running out over a footbridge, or traverse down in zigzag fashion. We elect to schuss—following Sverre, who tucks his poles under his arms and, in a bent-knee, half-squatting position, leaps over the edge and down, crossing the bridge far below, where he turns around and watches. It becomes a game—to see how close we can come to him.

What we don't realize from above is that some of the snow has melted off the bridge, leaving a rather narrow pathway to follow. Not hitting it precisely means a sudden stop. You can't see the bare wood until you are committed, and then it is too late to turn. One of the men is off the track and tries to turn. He skims by the open end of the bridge and drops off the bank, just missing the stream. He climbs up and waves his poles at us, then skis across the bridge to join Sverre. I decide to put my braking technique to a test and ride my poles down, holding them to one side. I slow down enough to direct my skis toward the patch of snow at the entrance to the bridge. Then I am through and across.

The trail follows the stream, skirting woods on one side. Sverre says, "We are on the golf course, you know." But there's no way of knowing. So much snow has fallen that the landscape has turned into gently rounded snowy curves. There are no sharp angles; even the banks of the stream are soft hummocks with a trickle of rippling water passing between them. There is nothing to remind us that we are skiing on a man-made playground; it is all one with the mountains and fields we have skied this morning.

To compensate for the schuss down, there is a rather steep but short climb up. We are totally in shadow now as we herringbone up the slope, knowing that from the top of it we will be able to see Sverre's house. This last climb is a struggle. We are more tired than we thought possible or care to admit. Skis slip, fatigue makes us awkward, but we really don't care. Toward the top some of us side step; our wax no longer prevents us from slipping back, even in a herring-bone.

But there it is—Sverre's house, less than a quarter of a mile away. It is all straight skiing now, and, out of pride, we try to finish with our best form. We stride slowly and change to double pole to push us along. Some have slowed down to a walk. And then we are home. It is twilight and the lights are on in his workshop.

The rucksacks come off and the skis are placed against a wall. Some of the party hurry to their cars, and others file into Sverre's place for a drink. I sip his Scotch, my body in a glow of tiredness, luxuriating in the feeling of satisfaction from a day that couldn't have been more complete. "It was something special," Sverre says. I can't help but agree.

Appendix

Appendix

WHERE THERE'S SNOW, THERE'S CROSS-COUNTRY: A BRIEF SKI-TOURER'S GUIDE

In using this listing of cross-country centers, readers should be warned that the material contained herein was correct up to press time, but could change. It is suggested that phone numbers, where given, be checked before calling.

NORTHEAST

VERMONT

BLUEBERRY HILL FARM
Located in the heart of Green Mountain National Forest. More than 10 miles of trails to explore. Contact Blueberry Hill Farm, Brandon, Vt.

163

BURKE MOUNTAIN

A historic cross-country center that goes back to the early days of skiing. Lessons, rentals. About 20 miles of trails. Contact Burke Mountain Ski Area, East Burke, Vt. 802-626-3305.

MT. SNOW

Marked trails. Instruction. Equipment and clothing for sale, equipment for rent. Contact Mt. Snow Ski Area, Vt. 802-464-3333.

RAWSONVILLE

Extensive ski touring at Cracker Barrel Ski Shop. Rentals, instruction. Some 50 miles of trails in the Magic Mountain–Stratton vicinity. Clothing and other gear for sale. Contact Woody's Cracker Barrel, Rawsonville, Vt. 802-824-5556.

STOWE

The Trapp Family Lodge. More than 40 miles of trails plus a Nordic ski school. Workshops throughout the season. Equipment and clothing for rent or sale. Contact Trapp Family Lodge, Stowe, Vt. 802-253-7545.

SUGARBUSH

Norwegian ski school operated by the Sugarbush Inn. Rentals. Clothing and equipment for sale. Picnic tours. Contact Sugarbush Inn, Sugarbush, Vt. 802-496-3301.

VIKING SKI TOURING CENTER

Prepared trails and rentals in the heart of Vermont. Contact Viking Ski Touring Center, Londonderry, Vt.

WOODSTOCK

At the Woodstock Inn, the ski touring center offers rentals, workshops, and instruction. All-inclusive Nordic Ski Week packages are also offered at reduced rates. Contact Woodstock Inn, Woodstock, Vt. 802-457-1100.

MAINE

SUGARLOAF

About 8 miles of prepared trails. Instruction, equipment rental. Contact Sugarloaf Ski Area, Sugarloaf, Me.

New York

LAKE PLACID
A trail network of 30 miles available. Expert touring on Mt. Marcy. Rentals at most local ski shops. Contact Lake Placid Tourist Bureau, Lake Placid, N.Y.

ROCHESTER
Many parks and trails. Rentals. Contact ABC Sport Shop, Rochester, N.Y.

TICONDEROGA
Many miles of trails in the vicinity of Ticonderoga. Rentals. Contact Bob's Skee Way, Ticonderoga, N.Y.

WEST

Touring in the Rockies is not the same as the typical cross-country skiing of the Northeast and Midwest. More technical competence is required to go into the high mountains; cross-country touring often becomes ski mountaineering. Instruction is available, however, at most ski centers and should be taken before any attempts are made to plunge into the mountains. Guided trips are preferable.

Colorado

ASPEN
A great deal of touring is available at Aspen, Aspen Highlands, and Snowmass. Tours take the skier into the Maroon Bells, 30 miles of trails in the vicinity of Snowmass, etc. Contact The Outdoor Sportsman, 303-925-3288, or Snowmass at Aspen, 303-925-2080.

STEAMBOAT SPRINGS

Ski packages include meals, housing, and instruction in cross-country and ski mountaineering. Equipment rental and sales. Contact Scandinavian Lodge, Steamboat Springs, Colo. 303-870-0517.

VAIL

Instruction, equipment sales, and rentals with extensive touring near the Gore Range. Contact Vail Associates, Vail, Colo. 303-476-5601.

WYOMING

JACKSON HOLE

Long tours are available in the Tetons. Equipment rentals and sales. Instruction. Contact Hostel-X or Teton Village, both in Jackson, Wyo.

CALIFORNIA

YOSEMITE NATIONAL PARK

Winter trips are led by the Yosemite Mountaineering School. Instruction and equipment available. Contact Yosemite Lodge, Yosemite National Park, Calif.

OTHER CROSS-COUNTRY CENTERS

An updated listing of all of the cross-country centers in the United States is contained in the *Ski Touring Guide,* Ski Touring Council, Inc., West Hills, Troy, Vt. It has complete details of routes available to cross-country skiers in every region of the country. Trail lengths are given, as are altitude variations and grading by ability. The guide costs $1.00.

Additional information on ski-touring throughout the United States and Canada is available from:

EAST AND NORTHEAST

American Youth Hostels, 315 Pearl St., Hartford, Conn. 06101
Brattleboro Outing Club, Brattleboro, Vt. 05301.
Eastern Division, Ski Touring Council, Inc., Rudolf F. Mattesich, West Hill Rd., Troy, Vt. 05868.
Jug End Barn, South Egremont, Mass. 01258.
Metropolitan New York Ski Touring Council, George Froehlich, 51–01 39th Ave., Long Island City, N.Y. 11104.
Mohonk Mountain House, New Paltz, N.Y. 12561.
Nordic Ski Shop, Williston, Vt. 05495.
Northern Light Village, Scandinavian Ski Shop, Phoenicia, N.Y. 12464.
Pleasant View Lodge, Freehold, N.Y. 12431.
Salisbury Winter Sports Club, Salisbury, Conn. 06068.
Williams Lake Hotel, Rosendale, N.Y. 12472.

MIDWEST AND WEST

Chairman, Central Division, Ski Touring Council, Inc., 4437 First Ave. South, Minneapolis, Minn. 55409.
Chairman, Rocky Mountain Division, Ski Touring Council, Inc., Mount Werner Training Center, Steamboat Springs, Colo. 80477.

NORTHWEST (Cascades)

Ray Courtney, Cascade Corrals, Stehekin, Wash. 98852.

CANADA

For touring in Glacier National Park, Mt. Assiniboine, Banff, Yoho National Park, and other Canadian Rocky Mountain areas in Alberta and British Columbia, contact Hans Gmoser, 132 Banff Ave., P.O. Box 583, Banff, Alberta, Canada.

SCANDINAVIA

Most touring centers in Sweden and Norway offer instruction, guided tours, equipment, and rentals. Thoroughly annotated maps of all of the routes in each country are available from the national ski clubs.

For information on ski-touring in these 2 countries—resorts, hotels, costs, package plans—contact the Swedish or Norwegian National Travel Offices. Both are located at 505 Fifth Ave., New York, N.Y. 10017. Another excellent source of information, especially on travel and package plans, is SAS Scandinavian Airlines, 555 Fifth Ave., New York, N.Y. 10017.